GLANCING BACK AT . . .

CLINTON

AND NEIGHBORING COMMUNITIES

including Clark Mills, Kirkland, Franklin Springs, and Hamilton College

"THE WAY IT USED TO BE"

Compiled by **Annette Foley, John Menard, David Dupont**

Written by **Philip E. Munson, Mary B. Dever,
Milford Morris, Frank Lorenz,
Mary Elizabeth Fay Kimball**

Edited by **George Searles**

Typed by **Donna Evans Yando**

Published for the Clinton Central School District Foundation
by
The Vestal Press, Ltd.

DEDICATION

Courtesy of Olan Mills

Every community can boast of special people whose very presence make it a better place in which to live. Philip E. Munson is such an individual, and ever since the Clinton Central School District Foundation decided to create this book, Phil has been the project's principal mentor.

Getting the facts correct in a book filled with historical details can be done only by someone who truly knows the territory. As Village of Clinton Historian, former Village trustee, co-founder of the Clinton Historical Society, and editor of the Clinton Historical Society Newsletter for the past thirty years, Phil is fully in tune with how our area's communities were in the past and how they evolved into what they are today.

Phil was born in Oneida, but his family moved to Clinton when he was an eighth-grader. During his high-school days here, he performed in various drama productions and ushered at the Scollard Opera House. After graduating with the Class of 1930, Phil attended Hamilton College. In 1942 he married Clinton schoolteacher Helen Rowley. They are the proud parents of a son and two daughters: Philip K. Munson, Jean Munson Blodgett, and Mary Lynn Munson Gras. Phil retired from the Aero Space Division of Kelsey Hayes Company in 1975.

Without Phil there would be no book. He shared his pictures, postcards, slides, and — most important — his expertise. He wrote the text for more than half the book, assisted with several slide presentations to local groups, and attended meetings to help the committee with important decisions.

It is with great pride that the Clinton Central School District Foundation dedicates this volume to a very special person indeed: Philip E. Munson.

Library of Congress Cataloging-in-Publication Data

Glancing back at — Clinton and neighboring communities : the way it used to be / written by Philip E. Munson . . . [et al.] : edited by George Searles ; compiled by Annette S. Foley, John F. Menard, David Dupont.
     p. cm.
  ISBN 1-879511-13-4. — ISBN 1-879511-14-2 (pbk.)
  1. Clinton (N. Y.) — History — Pictorial works. 2. Clinton Region (N. Y.) — History — Pictorial works. I. Munson, Philip E. II. Searles, George. III. Foley, Annette S. IV. Menard, John F. V. Dupont, David.
F129.C65G53 1993
974.7'62—dc20
          93-20997
          CIP

Published for the Clinton Central School District Foundation by The Vestal Press, Ltd.,
320 N. Jensen Road, P.O. Box 97, Vestal, NY, 13851

ACKNOWLEDGEMENTS

Thanks so much to all the many people who helped make this book possible!

If it were not for those who provided photographs and postcards, there would be no pictures. If it were not for the writers, there would be no text. If it were not for the page sponsors and the folks who helped with other fund-raising, there would be no money to pay the publisher for production and printing. By its nature, a project such as this must involve dozens of individuals, all contributing their time and talents in various ways. We shall attempt to recognize as many as possible here.

Photographs and postcards were loaned by people from all the communities. The Clinton Historical Society made available all of their archives. Most of the other postcards came from the collections of Phil Munson, Don Foley, and Evelyn and Mel Edwards. In addition, many other individuals came forth with pictures and/or cards for our consideration. We regret that we could not use every item submitted, but we tried. And we certainly appreciated all the offers! The book is better because of Nannette and Jack Allen, Barbara and Chris Blatz, Carol and Bernie Burns, Eleanor and John Calidonna, Elizabeth Canfield, Barbara and Ken Crane, Cynthia and John Ellis, Dawn and Gill Goering, Marie Golden, Hazel and Don Gorton, Tish and Jim Hyde, Dorothy and David James, John Joseph, Frank Lorenz, Ray Martin, Steffen Moller, Barbara and Dick Owens, Tom Pavlot, Dorothy and Robert Rouillier, Don Stratton, Susan and Tim Suppe, Robert Tegert, Herbert Wentworth, and Dean White.

The authors are an exceptional group. Mary Dever, Town of Kirkland Historian, wrote the pages exploring the Park Row area; she helps us envision the era of trolleys, steeples, and "silent policemen." Phil Munson, Village of Clinton Historian, contributed the text for more than fifty pages, ranging from schools to churches, from the canal to mines, and more. He was "with us" from the beginning of the endeavor. Listening to and learning from Phil is a wonderful experience. Milford Morris, Clark Mills Historian, provided excellent coverage of Clark Mills and its fascinating early English community. Frank Lorenz, editor of Hamilton College publications, not only knows the College's history, but relates it in a captivating way. Mary Elizabeth Fay Kimball, retired Town Librarian and long-time Kirkland resident, supplied interesting historical background for the photographs taken there.

Recognition is also in order for the many volunteers who helped secure the necessary capital to meet our production costs. At the bottom of each page you will see the name of a sponsor who contributed to the book fund. Jim Rishel spent countless hours finding page sponsors, as did Fred Alteri, Jack Allen, and Christine Menard. This was the heart of the fund-raising effort. In addition, the Savings Bank of Utica made a major contribution. Bev and Fred Alteri sponsored a very successful dinner. Hamilton College was of great assistance in many ways. Betsy Espe has helped in all aspects, and Mike Debraggio continues to guide our marketing effort at the college.

Typing and layout were done by Donna Yando, who spent innumerable hours at her word processor. George J. Searles did a wonderful job as editor and proofreader. James B. Torrance made several promotional presentations to local groups, and was also an excellent "sounding board" in our many organizational meetings. Mel Edwards assisted in the selection of photographs and postcards for inclusion. Thanks also to Don "Red" Foley and Christine Menard, who contributed great ideas and lots of time and effort.

As a group and as individuals, we say "Thank You" to each and every one who helped with this endeavor. People make a community what it is, and we are blessed to have so many who care deeply, not only about helping our school system, but also about preserving our local history as well.

Happy reading!

Annette Foley
John F. Menard
David DuPont

FOREWORD

I lift my glass in a grateful toast
To those glorious days of the used-to-be
Days that live on in memory,
Bathed in a shimmering golden haze-
Our still remembered "olden days"!
John Irving Dillon

In 1993 we find ourselves in the last decade of the twentieth century. Thinking in terms of decades and centuries, rather than of weeks and months, has given to the members of our committee — and hopefully to the reader as well — an interesting and thoughtful perspective on the publication of this book. Our natural curiosity about the past and especially the rich history of our own communities has provided an important basis for the concept of this book. Through the media of old postcards and pictures, and the knowledge of local historians, we have put together a collection of backward glances — moments in time captured on camera — of "the way it used to be" in our communities years ago. The changes in an area may be scarcely noticed by people living there. But over time these alterations of the local environment can be dramatic. How many people today remember where the Liberal Institute was in Clinton, where Danceland was in Kirkland, or the train station in Clark Mills? How many are familiar with the Park Hotel, a landmark in our area for over a century?

In taking this journey into the past, we have made our selections from hundreds of old postcards and photographs provided by many local residents. Postcards became available 100 years ago in 1893 when the U.S. Postal Service first approved unsealed letters for mail delivery. Their popularity increased quickly and soon every city, village, and town had pictures of its most prominent landmarks on postcards. Not only did people find it very convenient to send these cards to friends, but many people made postcard collections, a hobby still popular today. There is much that is not available on postcards, however, so there are also many photographs included in this book. Some of these photographs date as far back as before the Civil War.

The making of this book has been an enjoyable undertaking and we are the richer for it. Now when we walk down Park Row we cannot help but picture horses in front of the Clinton House Hotel, or hear the sounds of the trolley going around the village green, or see the red dust of iron ore in the streets as wagons make their way from the mines to the iron works in Franklin Springs. For some readers this book will bring back memories of time gone by; for others it will be a new journey through our local history; for all we hope it will be an enjoyable stroll through our rich local past, "those glorious days of the used-to-be."

This is the earliest known picture of West Park Row. Buildings beyond the Clinton House, north of today's alleyway or tunnel, were entirely destroyed by fire in 1862. Those from the College Street corner, including the original Clinton House, were destroyed in another of Clinton's major fires, this one in 1872. All were rebuilt and remain much the same today. (photo 1857)

This photograph shows the West Park Row area prior to the 1872 fire. In the area beyond the Clinton House are two "new" buildings erected following the 1862 blaze. The vacant spot between the two structures became the site of the new Tower Block, later the Scollard Opera House, erected in 1870. The three-story brick block at the far end on North Park Row was finished in 1868 and destroyed by fire in 1989. (photo circa 1869)

❦ Compliments of MacDonald-Yando Insurance Agency ❦

2

Both of these pictures show the July 13, 1887 Centennial Celebration. There was a mile-long parade, highlighted by the presence of 50 year old President Grover Cleveland and his bride of one year, Frances Folsom. (Note the photographers on top of the Hogan [Ives] Block.) Decorations filled the village and banners were strung across all the streets leading out of the Park. Across Water Street (Kirkland Avenue) the banner read, "Welcome to Our President." The remaining five street banners were "Welcome to the Oneidas"; "Foot, Blodgett, Bronson, Pond, Mrs. Hovey, Sherman — Our Pioneers"; "Forest to Farms"; Village of Schools"; and "1787 Clinton 1887."

More than 15,000 people jammed Clinton streets to watch the parade and take part in other festivities from band concerts to fireworks, which made the celebration a long-remembered one.

❦ Compliments of Clinton Lions Club — We Serve ❦

This house was built in 1820 by Othniel Williams, father of Othniel S. Williams, and remained in the Williams family until the 1930's. Remodeled in the 1870's, it was the site of the reception for President and Mrs. Grover Cleveland at the Clinton Centennial Celebration on July 13, 1887, when myriads of visitors swarmed over the front yard to shake the President's hand. Most recently the house has been the location of the Alexander Hamilton Inn. (photo 1887)

This centennial photograph of 26 Utica Street shows the home of Rev. and Mrs. Richard Cleveland, parents of Grover Cleveland, who resided here during the early 1850's. It was here that Grover Cleveland lived in 1851 while attending the Clinton Grammar School on College Street. A bronze Clinton Historical Society plaque, dedicated in 1968, marks the house. (photo 1887)

❦ In appreciation of a Great Community—The Lorne Bradbury & William Dandridge Families ❦

4

This view from East
Park Row looking
west includes the
Presbyterian Church,
Allen Block (with fire
alarm on the roof),
and to the left of the
church, the original
Kennedy Block,
which then housed a
trolley-terminal
lunchroom operated
by Carl Brockway and
Arthur J. Thomas. The
trolley had evidently
just arrived from
Utica, and incoming

passengers are about to board the Waterville-Clinton bus. Just beyond the bus is one of Clinton's early taxis. This block
was gutted by fire in October 1922. (photo 1921)

This photo, of South Park Row
looking east, shows the Park
Hotel on the right, along with
the Kennedy Block next door,
which had been recently
rebuilt after the fire of 1922. At
that time the building housed
the Matoon Motor Sales,
dealer in Willys-Knight, Nash,
and Overland automobiles.
Note the gasoline pump in
front. Meeting the trolley was
one of Clinton's twenty-four
licensed taxi cabs of that year.

The building, now known as the Vona Block, became the home of Marsette A. Vona's Clinton Shoe Center in 1956. (photo
1925).

❦ In memory of Marsette A. Vona, Sr. ❦

This South Park Row picture records the arrival of the first trolley to Clinton from Utica. Loaded with dignitaries from Utica, New Hartford, and Clinton, the trolley was greeted with cheers from the crowd of spectators, the ringing of church bells, and music by Bergman's Band from Utica, who appropriately played the contemporary tune, "I've Waited, Honey, Waited Long for You." After an official photograph, all sojourned to the nearby Wirth House for lunch. This marked the beginning of Clinton/Utica trolley service, which would continue until March 31, 1936. (photo 1901)

In this photo a trolley is standing at the southerly end of the Village Green prior to completing its circuit of the Park and returning down Utica Street to Utica's Union Station. During the 1920's and 1930's, the trolley was still the principal mode of transportation between Clinton and Utica. Meeting these half-hourly arrivals and departures were numerous Clinton taxicabs, most individually owned. Several had their own telephones attached to poles near the south end of the Village Green, one of which is visible alongside the trolley. Each phone had a loud bell with a distinctive tone recognizable by the owner, enabling patrons to contact their favorite cab. (photo 1930)

6

Opened in 1883 as the Willard House, this South Park Row landmark was constructed by Russell Willard on the spacious homestead of Orrin Gridley, once considered the richest man in town. The hotel went through five name changes and twenty-six proprietors during its seventy-eight years. It served as, among other things, a mecca for New York City visitors enjoying the bucolic charm of a Clinton summer or seeking a "fresh air" cure for health problems. The upper photo shows it as the Wirth House (1894-1904), the lower one as the Park Hotel (circa 1940)

❦ Compliments of Judy Welch ❦

Known since 1904 as the Park Hotel, this South Park Row hostelry was destroyed by fire on January 11, 1961. Over the years, it had become more of a place for apartment dwellers rather than transients. In 1923, the lower floor right became the meat market of the O'Brien brothers, James and John (or, as they were more familiarly known, Jim and Jack). After James's death in 1944, Mrs. James (Elizabeth) O'Brien, along with Edward Huther, continued the business until 1957 whereupon Mrs. O'Brien remodeled the premises and opened a popular women's apparel shop aptly named Elizabeth's. When the building was finally demolished in 1962, the site became a parking lot — not, however, until after a major oil company had unsuccessfully sought to erect a gasoline station on the corner. (photo 1961)

❦ Compliments of Elizabeth O'Brien Canfield ❦

121—The Park, Clinton, N. Y.

The Village Park has always been a gathering place for special programs and entertainment. If this photo could talk, it would tell tales about the activities in the "Old White Meeting House" on the south end, as well as the "regimental days" with all their flourishes. Historic monuments, a buried time capsule, a flagpole, and a scenic fountain adorn this beautiful area of the village. (photo 1908)

Once the site of School District No. 4's schoolhouse, the house on the right was purchased and remodeled after 1875 by E. S. Benedict for use as his home. By the time of this photo, it had become the property of Fred A. Root, but it was best known later on as belonging to Dr. Arthur Gaffney, who used the downstairs for his offices, renting out the second floor as an apartment. (photo 1910)

❦ Sponsored by Clinton Coiffures — Marie Golden ❦

The Clinton Methodist Church, on East Park Row, seen from the Park in this photo, was dedicated on January 1, 1842, thanks mainly to the efforts of Walter I. Gillespie. In 1868, it was extensively remodeled to its present form, acquiring a steeple and bell. In 1966, this church was sold to the Kirkland Art Center, as the Methodists had outgrown these premises and erected a new church on Utica Road. (photo 1955)

This East Park Row house is believed to have been built by Nathaniel Griffin about 1830. In this photo, the property was owned by Albert Brown, a Utica hotelier. In the 1940's it became the funeral home of William Walsh. On January 15, 1946, the business was purchased by Edward C. Heintz and his brothers, and since that time has remained in the Heintz family. The gentleman in the sleigh is Nathan Hayes, then president of Hayes Bank. (photo 1910)

❦ In Memory of Edward C. Heintz, 1921-1990 ❦

At the north end of the village, facing the Park, stood the Old Village Tavern, built by Deacon Isaac Williams in 1800. It later became the "Park House." Two of the later owners were Philander Budlong and John W. Bellinger, who retired in 1887, ending its use for hotel purposes. John E. McBride purchased this historic site in 1899 and had it razed, removing a landmark almost a century old. Indications are that the first meeting of the Board of Trustees of Hamilton College was held in this tavern on July 14, 1812. Lumbard Hall was erected on this site in 1926. (photo circa 1880)

THE PARK HOUSE.—This hotel was built at the northern end of the Village Park in the summer of 1800, and for a number of years was the only hotel in the village. During the Centennial celebration in July, 1887, it was used as a museum for the display of historic articles of local interest, and soon after was torn down.

HISTORIC CLINTON, No. 1.

This brick building, west of the Park House and facing the Park, was built as a store by Benoni Butler in 1826, and so remained through several owners. In 1878 it became the home of the Clinton Fire Department, which remained here until 1895 and then moved to the Williams Street side of the Onyan (Allen) Block. This photo depicts the uniformed members with some of their equipment, along with the Community Band. (photo 1887)

❦ Compliments of the Menard Family: Christine, John, Elizabeth, & Sarah ❦

In this photo of North Park Row is seen Peter Fake's general merchandise store, then under the ownership of his son, Augustus, who used his name, A. Fake, facetiously in his ads. It had successive owners until about 1922 when it was razed to erect the new Fire House. (photo 1880)

Lumbard Memorial Hall, built on the site of the former Park House and the Butler store, was dedicated on September 10, 1926. Designed by a Clinton architect, Arthur L. Easingwood, it owes its existence to a generous bequest of $42,900 from Ralph S. Lumbard, a local philanthropist. The home of village and town offices since its inception, it also housed the Clinton Post Office from 1926 until 1989. (photo circa 1926)

❦ Courtesy of Dick and Jean Williams ❦

This bronze figurine of a sea urchin was erected in the Village Green fountain in 1939 by the Houghton Seminary Alumnae Association as a memorial to their school, which existed in Clinton from 1861 to 1903. The statue, a work of American sculptor Edward Berge of the Grand Central Gallery (New York City), was installed in a new fountain designed by R. Clement Newkirk, a Utica architect. It was placed so that the right arm of the figure pointed toward the former school, which had been located on so-called Houghton Hill at the westerly end of Chestnut Street. Due to disrepair over the years, the fountain underwent a major facelift and on July 8, 1992, was rededicated by Mayor Richard Williams.

West Park Row once had two-way traffic, with parallel parking on one side and horizontal on the other. From L to R, merchants of that day were Hogan's (the popular soda fountain and news shop), The Grand Union Superette grocery, Charles Cone, (clothing and shoes), Turnock & Owens (furniture), Tom Yacano's Sweet Shop, Harold Ford's market, the A & P grocery, variety store of Guy Lewis, Clarence Weaver's liquor store, the Market Basket (a grocery operated by Harry Wesseldine), J. W. Delahunt's Rexall drug store, the Victory Chain grocery, and still another grocery, H. W. Roberts' Nation-Wide. Six groceries within a hundred yards certainly gave shoppers a choice! (photo circa 1939)

❦ Compliments of Jim and Rose Maier and Family ❦

This photo shows the Hayes National Bank as it appeared after it was completely remodeled inside and out, including a new concrete façade. The 1931 Ford sedan on the right belonged to Robert U. Hayes, president of the bank, who stands with other employees near the front entrance. (photo 1932)

Established in 1870, The Clinton Bank was transferred to Hayes & Company in 1878. In 1896, the bank moved from East Park Row to the remodeled brick Seth Hastings homestead on Kirkland Avenue, built about 1808. The Skenandoa Club occupied the upper floor in 1897 and remained there until 1965. Men standing in front of the bank in this photo are unidentified except for two in the rear row (James L. Burns, Sr., on the left, and Arthur W. Scoones on the right) and one in the front row (William Restle in the straw hat).

When the Fire Department made an addition to its building in 1927, the wooden structure facing Kirkland Avenue and housing Dawes' Meat Market was torn down. Space was allotted in the rear, however, enabling Dawes' Market to continue its business for another twenty years. The exterior was bricked over, concealing the history behind its walls. This photo shows the Hayes Bank at that time. (photo 1927)

438—CENTRAL FIRE STATION, CLINTON, N. Y.

The Clinton Fire Department building, which faces North Park Row, was erected in 1921 at a cost of $15,000. It was funded in part by a bequest from Ralph S. Lumbard, who also furnished money for Lumbard Memorial Hall. Prior to relocating here, the Department had been housed in the Onyan (Allen) Block on Williams Street. (photo 1932)

❦ Clinton Hose Company — Clinton Fire Department ❦

This 1930 photo taken in front of the North Park Row fire house displays all the department equipment at that time. On the far left is a new hook and ladder truck and on the far right is a new pumper, both purchased that year. In the center is the fire company's first motorized pumper, built in 1923 on a converted 1914 Pierce-Arrow automobile chassis. Though it performed well at fires, there were sometimes problems getting it there, due to lack of tractive power.

This photo depicts the Clinton Fire Department's old-fashioned handpump parked on Williams Street, alongside the Onyan (Allen) Block, where the Department was then headquartered. This pumper is now on display at the Department's Museum in Fire House #2 on Franklin Avenue.

❦ Clinton Hook and Ladder Company — Clinton Fire Department ❦

16

Post Office Block, Clinton, N. Y.

The central brick building in this view of North Park Row was erected in 1868 by Samuel Sherman, a local undertaker and livery stable operator. The plastered brick structure on the right, the future location of the Clinton Fire Department, dates to 1832, and the wood structure on the left, now the Burns Insurance Agency, dates to the 1790's. The three-story brick structure was destroyed in the spectacular fire of July 4, 1989, and was rebuilt in 1992. Note the trolley tracks in the foreground. (photo 1905)

This photograph of the Clinton Post Office interior was taken early in the century. At that time the post office was located on North Park Row, as it had been since 1872. In 1926 the post office was moved to the newly built Lumbard Hall. In this photo are O. J. Burns, postmaster, who is standing in the lobby, and Gaylord Ward, behind the window. (photo 1920)

🍎 The Burns Agency—Doing Business in Clinton Since 1919 🍎

This December 1913 photo taken in front of the post office on North Park Row shows the staff, including the rural carriers, about to start out to deliver holiday mail. Rear Row: Fred E. Payne, postmaster (in doorway); Flora Brockway, Assistant; Edna B. Swartz; Camella O. Payne. Second Row: L. N. Brockway, Charles Griffin, E. Payson Ellenwood, Gaylord D. Ward. Front Center: J. H. Libbey.

Known for much of its life as the Scollard Opera House, this block was built in 1870 by John H. Tower, who sold it to Dr. James Scollard in 1876. Originally erected with a peak roof, it was extensively remodeled in 1885 to include a dormer-windowed mansard roof, stained glass windows, an iron balcony, and an ornamental ironwork "Opera House" sign.

During its heyday, the second floor auditorium was the community center for town meetings, school graduations, theatrical presentations, dances, recitals, basketball games, and silent movies. Entrance to the auditorium was through the double doors at left. Other remembered occupants were J. W. Delahunt's drugstore, the Victory chain grocery, Fords Market, and — in the 1990's — a restaurant and the Clinton Shoe Center.

❧ Compliments of The Clinton Shoe Center—Jack and Mary Lane ❧

18

Thanks a Happy New Year from Cousin Mary

This overview of West Park Row looks south, with the Presbyterian Church as a focal point. The church, which was dedicated February 14, 1878, had a new bell installed on April 6, 1880, and a town clock the following week. The business blocks, rebuilt after the fires of 1862 and 1872, appear virtually the same today. The spire beyond the row of buildings is that of the Universalist Church on Williams Street, until recently the Masonic Temple. Built in 1870, the spire was destroyed by a violent windstorm in 1893. (photo 1880)

Though many businesses had changed hands, this 1910 West Park Row view, looking north, appears much the same as it had thirty years before (view above), except for the trolley tracks circling the Park, telephone and electric light poles, and a new roof, from peak to mansard, on the Scollard Opera House. It's important to note that the Clinton Pharmaceutical Company, now Bristol-Myers Squib, had its beginning in 1887 on the second floor of the then Robinson Block, now the site of Brooks Drugs. It moved to Syracuse in 1889. (photo 1910)

4—West Park Row, Clinton, N. Y.

❦ Sponsored by Mary B. Dever ❦

THE ALEXANDER HAMILTON INN — CLINTON, NEW YORK
THE HOME OF HAMILTON COLLEGE — ON ROUTE 12B — UTICA 8 MI.

Shortly after the Othniel S. Williams home on West Park Row was sold, it became a restaurant, and on January 2, 1947, George and Martha Traub became owners of the Alexander Hamilton Inn. With its spacious and beautiful bedrooms for overnight guests and its antique-filled dining rooms where gourmet delicacies were served, it became a prosperous and famous inn. (photo 1950)

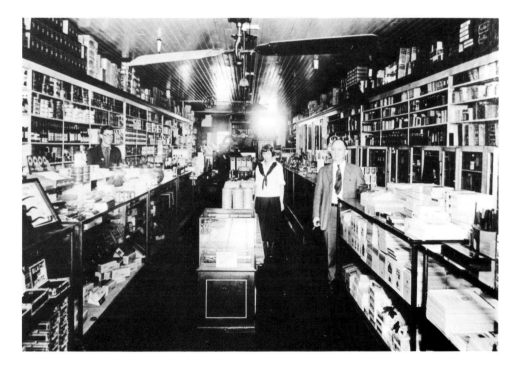

In this photo of Delahunt's Drug Store on West Park Row (now Clinton Shoe Center) one can see Emrys Owens standing behind the counter to the left. Clerk Doris Loomis is at center, while the owner J. W. Delahunt is standing on the right. Purchasing this business in 1917 from F. A. Root, Delahunt continued to run it until 1951, selling out to the Victory Chain who enlarged the store by including this drug store area. (photo 1925)

❦ Compliments of Dick & Barbara Owens ❦

20

West Park Row is shown here as a dirt road, with its hitching posts, horse-drawn vehicles, and a trolley from Utica approaching the south end of the Park. When trolleys first began serving Clinton in 1901, they came up the west side of the Park. They made their first stop opposite the Clinton House, thereby permitting passengers to use a crosswalk that stretched across the muddy road to the sidewalks beyond. After the introduction of automobiles and paved roads and the

1—West Park Row, Clinton, N. Y.

establishment of a taxi stand at the south end of the Park, the trolley route was changed. For safety reasons, cars then came up the east side, allowing travelers to alight and board in the Park, away from traffic. (photo circa 1907)

The Clinton House on West Park Row has an illustrious past. Built in 1805 by Joseph Stebbins, with a third story added in 1851, it was destroyed by fire in 1872. Rebuilt in 1875 by John H. Tower, it remained a well-known hostelry until the coming of Prohibition in 1920, when the lower floor was converted to a meat market by William H. Ford and the upper floors to flats or apartments. In 1987, it was extensively remodeled by Park Row Booksellers, Ltd., who converted the front to resemble the building as it originally appeared in the 1870's. (photo 1907)

❦ Compliments of Park Row Booksellers, Ltd. — Wolfe News Service, Inc. ❦

In the early 1900's the Clinton House was owned by Frank Blake. With the advent of prohibition he sold the property to William H. Ford, who remodeled the ground floor center into a meat market that remained at this location through son Harold and grandson Robert until 1963. In 1920 the store under the awning was occupied by Ferguson's Dry Goods. In 1930 it was taken over by Henry Brown, who combined it with his electrical store, which previously had been on Williams Street. It is currently the Cafe-on-the-Green. (photo 1912)

This more recent West Park Row photo shows the Park Row Pharmacy, which was owned by Robert Wagoner. He had purchased the block from the Taylor Estate in 1955. To the right is Stan's Coffee Shop, opened by Stanley Millard in 1945, which remained in business until 1979. In 1965, Donald Gorton relocated his Variety Store to the site shown in the photo. Later sold to Mr. & Mrs. Vincent Romanelli, it remained in existence

until 1986. The A & P store to the right of Gorton's followed Henry Roberts in the grocery business in 1934. All of the windows with "eyebrows" were part of the earlier Clinton House. (photo 1965)

❦ Sponsored by Charles & Irene Reed ❦

Here's West Park Row prior to the beautification effort of 1960, when all building fronts were painted white and all overhanging signs removed. It was on the second floor of the block above the Park Row Pharmacy that the Clinton Pharmaceutical Company, forerunner of present day Bristol-Myers Squibb, was founded in 1887. (photo 1955)

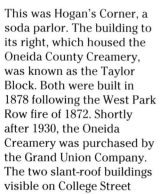

This was Hogan's Corner, a soda parlor. The building to its right, which housed the Oneida County Creamery, was known as the Taylor Block. Both were built in 1878 following the West Park Row fire of 1872. Shortly after 1930, the Oneida Creamery was purchased by the Grand Union Company. The two slant-roof buildings visible on College Street

were Bevivino's Shoe Repair Shop, later The Snip and Clip barber shop, and Frank Dempsey's property, demolished by the village in 1959 to make way for the College Street parking lot. (photo 1930)

❦ In memory of Esther Kennedy Welch, by Bernie Welch ❦

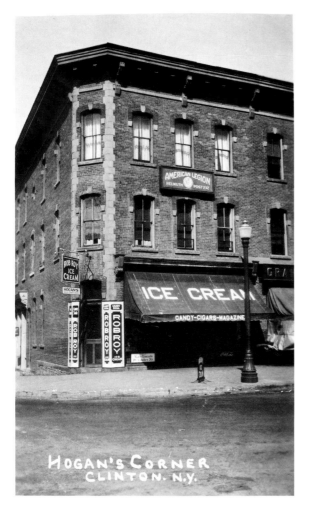

Hogan's Corner had earlier been the site of Moses Foote's home, later an inn and boarding house of Moses, Jr., son of the village founder. After the fire of 1872, Charles Ives erected a new building on the site, which in 1906 became the property of Timothy Hogan. From that date until 1959 it remained in the Hogan family as a corner store featuring tobacco products, confectionery, periodicals, and a famed soda fountain. (photo circa 1930)

This West Park Row photograph shows a small, unusual Great Atlantic & Pacific Tea Company store. Opened in 1934, it stayed in operation until 1969. A throwback to the family grocery store where customers were waited upon, it remained for years an anachronism in the huge A & P grocery chain after all other stores had become self-service supermarkets. Even the sign was inconsistent, since newer ones displayed nothing but an "A & P" logo. The sign above the alleyway advertised Robert H. Nichols' Oldsmobile Garage. The garage was located through the tunnel to the right rear, in a building built in 1914 from bricks and steel trusses from the Franklin Iron Company furnace which had been demolished the previous year. Mr. Nichols purchased the building in 1926. (photo 1955)

❦ The Hogans: Jane Ellen, Timothy, Sue Ellen, Mary Ann, Patricia & Michael ❦

This familiar building at the corner of College and Williams Streets was built in 1884 by William Onyan. It replaced a similar one constructed a year earlier that had been almost immediately destroyed by fire. In 1886 it became the home of H. J. Allen and Son hardware, a business that would remain there until 1977. Since 1904, it has been known as the Allen block. When erected, the building boasted an opera house on the third floor which proved unsuccessful due in part to a long flight of stairs required to reach it from a Williams Street entrance. From 1895 to 1938, the third floor was the Masonic Temple, home of Clinton Lodge #169. (photo circa 1890)

❦ Compliments of the Nannette and Jack Allen Family ❦

On the southern side of upper College Street, this brick block housing the Peter McCabe grocery store was built in 1866 as a hotel called The Hamilton House. The building purchased by Peter McCabe in 1898 became the home of the McCabe family grocery for the next 55 years. Today the block is owned by George Mair. (photo circa 1904)

This College Street building west of the Allen block was erected in 1883. It was purchased in 1953 by the Alteri family who opened a restaurant on the site; the building was destroyed by fire in 1963. Since rebuilt, it's still the home of Alteri's, a popular Clinton hostelry. (photo circa 1953)

❦ Compliments of Mr. and Mrs. Fred Alteri ❦

College St., Clinton, N. Y.

Having a fine time. Went to a Concert given by the Utica Chorus of forty voices last night. Wish you could both have heard it. With love Maud

Handcolored.

This postcard view is of Upper College Street. The building housing the livery stable was erected in 1886 by William Robinson, whose family continued to operate a livery on this site until 1917. At that time, the site was converted to accommodate another type of horsepower, becoming an automobile garage. (photo circa 1904)

Here's College Street looking west from the corner of Williams Street and West Park Row. The so-called "Silent Policeman," which stood at the intersection of these streets (ostensibly to aid traffic flow), consisted of a box with continuously flashing red lights on all sides, fitted on a pedestal anchored in a huge block of concrete. Many an unwary motorist discovered that it was immovable. It had a short life. (photo circa 1930)

ENTRANCE TO COLLEGE ST.

❧ Compliments of the Village Tavern - Jack and Laura Buschmann ❧

Today's Owens-Pavlot Funeral Home at 35 College Street was once the home and office of Dr. Roy B. Dudley and family. In 1934 it was purchased by Emrys and Emma Owens, who converted it to a funeral home. The rear portion, not visible, was probably built between 1800 and 1811 by Timothy Barnes, early clockmaker and maker of Clinton's first church bell. The front portion shown was constructed about 1843, with an extensive westerly wing added in 1955. Among the occupants in its long history have been a clockmaker, a potter, a college president, a carriage maker, two physicians, two ministers, and a funeral director. (photo circa 1905)

This is Upper College Street looking east from the Marvin Street corner. The house with the steps in the right corner of the photo (now #37) was then the home of Clinton architect Arthur L. Easingwood who designed (among many other buildings) Lumbard Hall and the firehouse. The building seen on the left, then owned by the Catlin family, was occupied by Dr. Conway A. Frost. The rear portion of this home was later moved by then-owner Hugh Larkin to the vacant lot

A 8762 College Street, Clinton, N. Y.

visible next west to become #26 College Street. Further up the street, the sign over the sidewalk marks the entrance to the Clinton Livery stable operated by Allen Turnock. He was the son of Matthew Turnock, the local undertaker, who was the precursor of today's Owens and Pavlot. (photo circa 1904)

❦ Continuous Service to Our Area since 1867 by Owens-Pavlot Funeral Service ❦

This building on the northern side of College Street forms the westernmost part of Brooks Drug Store, next door to the Old Apothecary Shop. Only the two bay windows and second floor balcony remain from the original building. Built in 1853 by John H. Tower, it became the home of Col. J. T. Watson's drug and provision store in 1859, and so remained in the Watson family until it closed in 1945. The window in the lower left corner is now part of today's Village Tavern. (photo circa 1875)

Shown here is the interior of Watson's Drug Store, College Street. Charles E. Watson, then the proprietor, complete with tailcoat, stands amid a jumbled array of merchandise including toilet paper (5 for 25¢), and a counter overflowing with stationery and school supplies, pens, pencils, pads, notebooks, etc. — even textbooks, then the purchase responsibility of students and their parents. (photo 1922)

❦ Compliments of Roy and Marilyn Smith ❦

Felix Stern's College Street Harness Shop is today the site of a health food store. Mr. Stern, in the apron, opened his store in 1896 and remained until 1952. In addition to making and repairing harnesses, he also handled luggage. The corner of the building to the left of the horse was Bartell's blacksmith shop which sat back about fifteen feet from the street and is today the rear portion of Bitteker's Electric. (photo circa 1910)

This is the exterior view of Peter McCabe's grocery store on College Street. The store then covered the entire front portion of the brick block today owned by George Mair. The girl in the cart is believed to be the late Catherine McCabe Spath, with her father, Peter McCabe, at her side. (photo circa 1910)

❦ Compliments of George Mair ❦

This building at 32 College Street, since 1980 the home of the Clinton Courier newspaper, was built by Owen J. Burns in 1885 as a grocery store. The business soon branched out to sell livestock feed, building supplies, carriages and harnesses. Burns erected the storehouse at the rear about 1900; it was dismantled in 1962. Progenitor of some of the local families of that name whose offspring have contributed much to the community, "O. J.," as he was popularly known, long advertised his business as "the Right Man in the Wrong End of Town." It remained in the Burns family — father, son, and grandson — until it closed in 1958. Pictured in the photograph, are O. J. Burns on the right, with his helper of that time, Walter Birge. (photo circa 1900)

❦ Sponsored by Owen J. Burns II and son, Owen J. Burns Jr. ❦

The interior of Burns Grocery at 32 College Street was typical of family-owned groceries of the period. Customers visiting the store would be waited on by a clerk; or if one preferred, a telephoned order would be delivered. Standing left to right: O. J. Burns, owner; Louis Burns (not related); Lynn Cackett; two unidentified people; and James L. Burns, Sr., son of O. J., who would succeed his father. (photo circa 1930)

On the corner of College Street and Franklin Avenue are State Routes 12B and 412 (the 7th shortest state highway in New York State) prior to the installation of traffic lights. Homestead Bank, built in 1975, now occupies the corner to the rear of the Route 412 sign, and the new United States Post Office, erected in 1989, is located in the area between the "Rok" on the right and the Shell Service station on the left. (photo circa 1962)

❦ The James & Alice Burns Family - Jim, Bernie, Jack, & Jean Burns Duffy ❦

This landmark at 36 College Street, built in 1864 as a grocery store, has spent most of its life as a dispenser of libations. It's been called the "Rok" since 1973. An employee is shown turning on the "air conditioning." (photo 1987)

This tally-ho coach from the Robinson Livery is carrying a load of passengers, possibly headed for Hamilton College, past the corner of College Street and Franklin Avenue in front of the building housing today's "Rok." (photo circa 1895)

❦ Compliments of the Rok — Mark Smith, Proprietor ❦

This gasoline service station of Jerry Schilling, who long personified "service" to a multitude of Clinton motorists, was originally opened by Jacob G. Schilling, his father, in 1928. Operated by the Schilling family for 46 years, it was sold in 1976. The building is located between Marvin Street and Franklin Ave. (photo circa 1978)

Looking down Franklin Avenue from College Street, the flood of June 21, 1905 is shown. A torrential rainfall that lasted for hours caused streams to overflow, including that portion of the old Chenango Canal west of Franklin Avenue and Meadow Street, creating flood waters that inundated not only Franklin Avenue, but College Street as far as the Kirkland Town Library. (photo 1905)

34

A College Street scene looking west shows the railroad track and crossing gate of the New York Ontario & Western Railway. If in existence today, the rails would bisect both the new Post Office and the Homestead Bank. The building at the photo's right edge was last known as the Keith Block. Located at the corner of Chenango Avenue, it was built in 1866 and demolished in 1961. During its existence, it housed many businesses on the ground floor, with apartments (or "flats" as they were then called) on the upper floors.

The building across from the Keith Block was built as a warehouse about 1864 on the Chenango Canal bank. In 1931, it became a tailoring and dry cleaning establishment and has so remained to this day, owned since 1974 by John Fehlner. Built like a parallelogram, it is one of Clinton's unique structures. (photo circa 1920)

Shown below is the eastern end of the Keith Block on College Street. In 1908 Wayne V. Keith and Son (Arthur) took over the coal business of Charles H. Smyth, which had occupied this same site since 1878. The canopy covered a scale where loads of coal from the large sheds in the rear were weighed prior to delivery to customers. The large sheds bordering Chenango Avenue were serviced by a New York Ontario & Western Railway spur, into which incoming loaded cars of coal were pushed up an incline to the upper floor of the coal trestle where they were dumped to the floor below. Erected in 1888, the trestle and sheds were torn down in 1968. (photo circa 1908)

Receding glaciers centuries ago left many kames or hillocks of sand and gravel throughout Central New York. One of these, long known as Christmas Knob because of the many evergreens that once graced its summit, is located on Norton Avenue at the lower end of Elm Street. The house that now crowns its top was built by Dr. Dorrance K. Mandeville, a local physician and Hamilton College graduate. Since completion in 1866, the house has been occupied by five families.

Erected in 1927, to replace an earlier mill on the same site, the Clinton Cider Mill has been an Elm Street landmark for nearly a century. Long a popular spot for young and old alike to watch apples converted to cider and to purchase the tasty result, it was enlarged in 1977. Its unique operation has prompted coverage by varied national publications, including the *New York Times Magazine*. The mill has been owned by the Wentworth family since its beginning in 1900. Harold Wentworth is the present third-generation proprietor.

🍎 Compliments of the Clinton Cider Mill 🍎

The Kirkland Town Library at the intersection of College and Elm Streets is seen in this postcard. Erected in 1871-72 as a chapter house for Hamilton College's first Greek letter society, Sigma Phi, it was sold in 1902 to the Kirkland Town Library Association. The large porch was added about 1906 and removed in 1929. (photo circa 1906)

The upper floor of the Kirkland Town Library looked like this early in the century. It was used at the time as a gymnasium by the Clinton Preparatory School, a private boy's school (1898-1913) then located on the site of today's Clinton Central Middle School. From 1960 to 1966, this space was the home of the Kirkland Art Center, and from 1966 to 1993, the Clinton Historical Society. (photo circa 1906)

❦ Compliments of John, Lois, Dan, Jeff, and Steve Lemmer ❦

A striking structure with its red brick facade and unique tower, the Sigma Phi chapter house (as it appeared shortly after construction) is now the Kirkland Town Library. Sigma Phi was the only Hamilton College fraternity to build in the village. Although it was erected by a local architect and builder, F. A. Smith, no records of the original plans have been located. (photo circa 1872)

Residence of Clinton Scollard. Clinton, N. Y.

This Queen Anne house at 70 College Street, now the home of John B. Allen, Sr., was erected in 1892. It was built for a Clinton native, Clinton Scollard, an English literature professor at Hamilton College who later became a nationally recognized author and poet. Local architect Arthur L. Easingwood, who was involved in several projects including Lumbard Memorial Hall, designed and built this home, which has been in the Allen family since 1918. (photo circa 1900)

❦ Compliments of the John B. Allen Family ❦

This postcard shows College Street looking east toward the village, just west of the Oriskany Creek bridge which is visible at center. College Street remained a dirt road until 1922 when a contract was awarded to construct a concrete road from the village line to Griffin Road atop College Hill at a cost of $52,804. (photo circa 1920)

A flour and feed mill was located on College Street on the west bank of the Oriskany Creek adjacent to the bridge. Built as a grist mill about 1820, it was enlarged and improved in 1891 to include modern rolling machinery capable of producing fine flours with such enticing names as "Splendid, " "White Satin," and "Snowflake." The mill was destroyed by fire in 1915. (photo circa 1900)

❧ Compliments of Fred, Judy, and Rick Wollin ❧

This is another view of the flour and grist mill taken from the easterly side of the Oriskany Creek near the College Street bridge. The arched bridge is to the right and the dam is at the left. (photo circa 1898)

Oriskany Creek and Mill, College Street.   Clinton, N. Y.

Looking south from College Street just west of the Oriskany Creek bridge, this view shows the mill pond. Created by the dam shown on page 40, it furnished power to the flour mill shown in the top photo and visible at the right edge of this picture. The small building is the mill's horse barn. During the summer, the pond was also sometimes used for recreational boating.

🍎 Compliments of the Class of 1943 🍎

40

A dam across the Oriskany Creek was located just south of the College Street bridge. Originally constructed about 1860 to replace an earlier, smaller one farther upstream, it furnished water power to the flour mill on the west bank near the bridge, as well as a planing mill that earlier occupied the east bank. It was dismantled after the fire that destroyed the flour mill in 1915. (photo circa 1900)

A 8759 The Dam, Clinton, N. Y.

Here the old Oriskany Creek bridge on College Street is seen from the creek bed looking south. The bridge, built of stone, was completed in 1860 at a cost of $1590. The three attractive arches were less so in the spring when ice floes, tree trunks, and other debris made a dam of the bridge, causing water to inundate College Street east and west and often requiring dynamite to break up the stoppage. The bridge was replaced by the present single-span structure in 1959. (photo circa 1910)

Oriskany Creek Bridge, College St., Clinton, N. Y.

❦ Compliments of Jim and Ann Torrance and family ❦

This view of the Chenango Canal looks south from the College Street bridge toward lock #19 in foreground and Franklin Springs. Though the photo is undated, the condition of the canal indicates that it may be close to the time the canal closed in 1878, perhaps even the early 1870's. At the right edge of the picture, note the towpath which today would be Chenango Avenue south. The bridge, from which the picture was taken, was removed in 1899 and replaced by the present stone culvert.

This view of the Chenango Canal looks north toward Kirkland Avenue from the College Street bridge at the same time as the above photo. The towpath is to the left, and the campus of Cottage Seminary is beyond the hedge bordering the towpath. The house in the distance with the chimney visible still exists today at 8 Kirkland Avenue, just north of the upper driveway of the Clinton House Apartments. Chenango Avenue closely follows the towpath and that part of the canal bed nearby. Also visible are railroad tracks beyond the shanty, as well as part of the present-day Agway in the distance.

❦ In Memory of Isabelle Howlett ❦

The original Clinton railroad station is shown above. The structure, originally a canal warehouse, was erected in 1847 adjacent to the Chenango Canal and the canal bridge on Water Street, now Kirkland Avenue. In use until a new passenger station was built in 1884, it was demolished in 1885. Spectators on the platform are evidently among those attending the dedication of the new station across the tracks on the opposite corner of Water Street. This old building occupied the same spot as today's Clinton House Apartments. (photo 1884)

This is an earlier photo of the railroad station which served the Utica, Clinton, and Binghamton Railroad. This railroad later became the New York Ontario & Western Railroad, whose single track, completed through Clinton in 1866-67, crosses the street in the foreground. The building beyond the bridge remains today as a residence at 8 Kirkland Avenue. (photo circa 1871)

❦ Compliments of the Searles family ❦

A crowd, including the Westmoreland band, gathered for the dedication of Clinton's new passenger station on May 26, 1884. Located on Water Street, now Kirkland Avenue, it occupied the area adjacent to the railroad historical marker near the easterly end of the present Agway establishment. A unique, slate-roofed structure with an arcade through the center, it remained in use until 1932, at which time passenger service on the Utica and Rome branches of the New York Ontario & Western Railroad was discontinued. Sold by the railroad, it became a storage warehouse; it eventually fell into disrepair and was torn down in 1944. (photo 1884)

Our citizens have done their part to help their country and in this scene near the New York Ontario & Western passenger station on Kirkland Avenue, well-wishers gather to bid farewell to local World War I recruits about to depart for Fort Dix, New Jersey. The cars would soon be attached to an incoming southbound train. (photo 1917)

❦ Compliments of V.F.W. Post 9591, Clinton, NY ❦

This is a photo of a two-horse bobsled with plow underneath used to clear village sidewalks of snow. (photo circa 1920)

Winter weather has always been a matter to deal with in Central New York. This ingenious model-T Ford roadster had skis in place of front wheels and an extra set of rear wheels joined to the drive wheels by a caterpillar tread arrangement. It was used by one of Clinton's rural mail carriers to combat snowy roads. This view shows it parked in front of the post office, then located on North Park Row in the building that was destroyed by fire in 1989. (photo 1925)

❦ Compliments of Ken Jones Snow Plowing ❦

This Town of Kirkland "Walters" snow plow battled to open Crow Hill Road near Chuckery Corners after the snow storm of February 1936. These trucks were very powerful for the time and were favorites of drivers who had to contend with heavy snow. The Town purchased its first one in 1927 and it became known as "Big Bertha," a name believed to have been associated with the wife of one of the drivers. (photo 1936)

An early motorized Town of Kirkland snow plow is shown on Elm Street. The driver standing next to the truck is Bill Jones who resided at 8 Elm Street. At the time, all motorized town equipment was stored in a barn at the rear of present-day 11 Elm Street. (photo circa 1926)

❦ Compliments of the George Marsh Family ❦

46

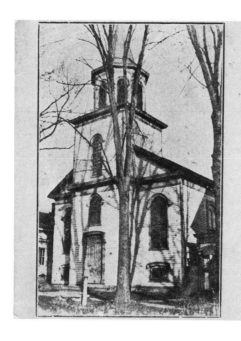

The Clinton Baptist Church
desires the pleasure of
your presence at the An-
nual Roll-call Service,
to be held in the Church
on Thursday evening, Jan-
uary 19, 1911, at 7:00
o'clock. If you cannot
be present, please send a
letter stating your
Christian experience, to
be read at such meeting;
after which there will
be a ten-cent supper and
a social hour.

S. J. Douglas, Pastor.

The Baptist Church on Fountain Street, the oldest remaining church structure in Clinton Village, was built in 1832. A steeple was added during extensive remodeling about 1870, but has since been removed. No longer in use for church services, the building was given to the Clinton Historical Society in 1993. (photo 1911)

St. James Episcopal Church on Williams Street was erected 1863-1865, and the adjoining rectory in 1884. Gothic Revival in style, it originally had a tall spire steeple which was destroyed in a violent windstorm in 1893 and never rebuilt. (photo circa 1920)

46

❦ In Retention of History — The Clinton Historical Society Inc. ❦

This, the original St. Mary's Roman Catholic Church, was erected at the corner of Marvin and Prospect Streets on the same site as the present structure. Dedicated in October, 1854, it was a wood structure and was used for services until 1909 when it was torn down to make room for a new church. (photo circa 1900)

The new St. Mary's Roman Catholic Church was dedicated in January, 1913. It was built of Medina sandstone and cost about $100,000. (photo circa 1913)

❦ Dedicated by Virginia and Maurice Page Sr. and Family ❦

48

Clinton's first church, the Congregational, was built on a mound at the southerly end of the Village Green in 1796, and was known as the White Meeting House. It was demolished in 1836 when a new Congregational Church was completed on the south side of the Green in that same year. (illustration 1796)

OLD HOME WEEK
Town of Kirkland

Town Church in 1796

August 16-23, 1902

The original Stone Church, erected in 1835-36 on South Park Row, was later to become Presbyterian.
Built of local limestone, it cost $8,000. It was destroyed by fire in 1876 along with the Mannering Block next door. Note the spire of St. James Church on Williams Street which shows over the roof of the corner structure. The building in the right corner is the Universalist Church, completed in 1870. Until recently the same building was the Masonic Temple. (photo 1870)

❧ Sponsored by a Member of Stone Presbyterian Church ❧

The Old Stone Church and Park Hotel. Clinton, N. Y.

The Presbyterian Church, popularly known as the Stone Church, is constructed of a local blue limestone which, when weathered, turns to a rich brown color. Erected in 1878 to replace the original Stone Church that occupied the same site, it was designed by Syracuse architect Horatio Nelson White and cost approximately $40,000. The 160-foot steeple was removed in 1923 for safety reasons. Until 1898, all Hamilton College graduation exercises were held in this church and its predecessor. (photo circa 1910)

This photo shows the Stone Presbyterian Church as it looked after removal of the steeple and remodeling of the tower in 1924. It appears much the same today. An interesting bronze plaque on the front of the church states in part that Clinton native Thomas Hastings (1784-1872) was once choir director of this local parish. He was a noted American composer and publisher of hymns, among them "Rock of Ages."

THE PRESBYTERIAN CHURCH, CLINTON, N. Y.

FOUNDED 1791

ORIGINAL "OLD STONE CHURCH"
DESTROYED BY FIRE 1876

CORNERSTONE LAID
1877

DEDICATED 1878

STEEPLE REMODELED
1924

50

441—METHODIST CHURCH. CLINTON. N. Y.

Built as the Methodist Episcopal Church in 1842, this building was extensively remodeled in 1867, at which time the present tower and steeple were added. In 1966 it became the home of the Kirkland Art Center when a new Methodist Church was constructed on Utica Road. (photo circa 1950)

The Lutheran Home started in 1920 when a group of Lutherans from Utica purchased the Henry Stappenbeck property on Utica Road and converted it into a home for the aged. Originally only the center portion of the building shown existed; the wings were added in 1932 and 1963. Today the building is part of a complex of several adjacent structures devoted to the care of the aged and handicapped. Except for Hamilton College, it is the largest employer in the Town of Kirkland.

The Lutheran Church Home for Aged and Infirm at Clinton, New York 171

❦ Sponsored by Bill and Bev Rudge ❦

The Old
White Seminary
Clinton, N. Y.

This building, erected in 1850 at the top of Williams Street, housed the female department of the Clinton Liberal Institute, a Universalist school that existed in Clinton from 1832 to 1878. It was popularly known as White Seminary in honor of the second preceptress, Miss E. R. White. It was here that Clara Barton, founder of the American Red Cross, attended school. The building, after use as a school, eventually became a rooming house for miners and, in great disrepair, was demolished in 1908. (photo circa 1890)

This house on Chestnut Street at the top of Williams Street was built by Edwin Fuller Torrey in 1908, and occupied the same site as the former White Seminary building. The pillars used were the only items from the original structure. Most of the remaining material from the demolished seminary building was utilized to build the Church of the Annunciation in Clark Mills.

❧ Compliments of Rhoda and Fuller Torrey ❧

Old Houghton Seminary, Clinton, N. Y.

The view of the entrance to Houghton Seminary shows the girls' school, which from 1861 to 1903 occupied this site at the westerly end of Chestnut Street. It was dismantled in 1912 to make way for the new home of John E. McLaughlin, a Utica businessman. The brick pillars bordering the entrance remain today. (photo circa 1890)

Students of Houghton Seminary take a break on the front lawn. The young lady with the bow and arrow may be taking aim at approaching Hamilton students, who on occasion were known to serenade the girls of Houghton. The house in the photo is not a seminary building but it is the next house east on Chestnut Street. (photo circa 1890)

❧ Compliments of Clinton Parent-Teacher Association ❧

Shown above is a front view of Cottage Seminary for young ladies, another of Clinton's many private schools of the 19th century. During its existence from 1862 to 1898, it occupied the same campus as the present-day Clinton Central Middle School, and probably had the most attractive campus of all the academies in town. In 1898, the buildings and grounds were taken over by Clinton Preparatory, a boys' school that remained on the site until 1913. (photo circa 1880)

Cottage Seminary, Clinton, N. Y.

Officers of Cottage Seminary Association

Miss Anna Moore, President

Miss Florence Hope,
Mrs. Henry Turnock, Vice-Presidents

Miss Lizzie Anderson,
Mrs. R. B. Dudley, Secretaries

Miss Susie Tibbitts, Treasurer

Here's another view of the buildings and campus of Cottage Seminary. Individuals listed on the postcard were the first officers of an alumnae association formed in 1907. All were Clintonians. (photo circa 1880)

❦ Dedicated to Barbara Anway ❦

If you don't have a hill, make one! This is a toboggan slide at the rear of the Clinton Preparatory School, a boys' school, which from 1898 to 1913 occupied the former Cottage Seminary buildings on the site of today's Clinton Central Middle School on College Street.

This is an interior view of a Clinton Preparatory School classroom. School desks are typical of the period. Though steam heat is evident, electric lights are yet to come. This building was on the site of the present Clinton Central Middle School. (photo circa 1903)

❧ Compliments of the Michael Moore Family ❧

The male department of the Clinton Liberal Institute occupied the southeast corner of Mulberry and Utica Streets. Erected in 1832 of native stone, it contained both dormitories and classrooms, and was so used until the Institute moved to Fort Plain in 1878. After the move, the building eventually became a warehouse and rooming house of sorts. In disrepair, it was sold in 1903 to Hamilton College, which tore it down and used the stone to build Carnegie dormitory. Leland Stanford of California fame, was once a student here. This photo was taken from the Mulberry Street "Knob". (photo circa 1870)

Dwight's Rural High School was erected in 1857 by the Rev. Benjamin W. Dwight on the southwest corner of Elm Street and Norton Avenue, in the general area of today's University Manor. Although it was originally a school for boys, a number of girls were admitted in 1862. It was destroyed by fire in 1865 and never rebuilt. After the fire, male students were transferred to the Clinton Grammar School, and females to Houghton Seminary. (photo circa 1860)

❧ Compliments of the Clinton Teachers Association ❧

56

The Clinton Grammar School, a private secondary
school chartered by New York State, was founded in
1813 and moved into this College Street building in
1816. During its existence, it occupied a space that today
would be the rear yards of Nos. 86 and 88 College Street.
It originally comprised just the part with the sloped roof;
the tower and the porch were added during extensive
renovation in 1866. The school closed in 1892 when it
was combined with the Clinton High School on Marvin
Street. The building was torn down in 1899. It was here
that Grover Cleveland attended school.

High School. Clinton, N. Y.

Erected in 1892-93, this Marvin Street building was built to accommodate a growing local public school population.
Though it was called Clinton High School, it contained all the elementary grades as well (on the ground floor). After the
completion of the new high school on College Street in 1933, the building was used for elementary classes only.
Condemned for further school use in 1976, it has since been converted to living quarters, and is now known as the Marvin
Street School Apartments.

❧ Compliments of the Clinton School Alumni Association ❧

This huge elm tree in the rear yard of the Clinton Preparatory School was still in existence behind today's Clinton Central Middle School when the building was completed in 1933. Despite care, the elm finally succumbed to Dutch Elm disease and had to be removed. A landmark of sorts, it was probably the largest tree in the village. (photo circa 1905)

The Clinton Central Junior-Senior High School, now the Clinton Central Middle School, owes much of its attractive campus to the Cottage Seminary and the Clinton Preparatory School, which once occupied the same spot. Various trees, such as the one in the foreground, date back to the earlier campus. The tree showing on the right behind the school is none other than the huge elm in the photo above.

CLINTON CENTRAL JUNIOR-SENIOR HIGH SCHOOL

Erected on former site of Cottage Seminary at an approximate cost of $350,000. Corner Stone laid 1932. Dedicated 1933. Auditorium seats about 750 people.

❦ In memory of Margaret Moore ❦

58

The new Clinton High School was built at the rear of the former Junior-Senior High School, now the Middle School. This aerial photo shows construction under way. (photo 1964)

This aerial view of the spacious Clinton Central School campus shows the present Middle School, built in 1933, in the foreground, with the Elementary School, erected in 1957, at the upper right. In 1990, the High School and Middle School were physically linked by an addition constructed in the space between the two buildings at the extreme left of the photo. (photo 1966)

❦ In memory of Marjorie Bryden ❦

Shown here is the outdoor skating rink on Franklin Avenue. Constructed in 1926, this facility was open during the winter months until 1948, when the first Clinton arena was erected. Located on the point between Franklin Avenue and Meadow Street in the general area of Dey Chevrolet, it furnished winter recreation for hundreds of children and adults alike, who changed their skates in the warmth of the stove-heated shanty at the rear. It was also the home of the Clinton High School hockey team and the Clinton Hockey Club, forerunner of the Clinton Comets. These teams often played before crowds of several hundred

spectators who stood in bone-chilling weather atop snow banks that lined the side boards. Enjoying an afternoon of skating are (from left to right) James Sherman and his daughters Catherine Sherman Morgan and Ann Sherman Yozzo, friends Virginia Stanley and Mary Lou Stanley MacPherson (both nieces of the late Ed Stanley), and one unidentified skater. (photo 1930)

The late Wilfred "Red" Goering, standing by the sideboards of the outdoor ice rink on Franklin Avenue, is shown with some of the ice-cleaning equipment of that day: brooms and snowshovels. Then a high school senior and goalie on the hockey team, he is wearing the typical, male high-school winter outfit, then very popular: wool plus-four knickers, argyle socks, a heavy maroon Block "C" crew- neck sweater, lined leather mittens, (sometimes called "Skunkin mitts"), and on his feet something no well-dressed student would be without — cloth-topped, four-buckle galoshes flopping and clinking as one walked, and never, ever buckled. (photo 1926)

❦ In memory of Wilfred "Red" Goering, compliments of Gill & Dawn Goering ❦

This interior view of the original Clinton Arena shows a capacity crowd on opening night, February 13, 1949. Spectators saw the Clinton Hockey Club, forerunner of the Clinton Comets, play New York-Ontario League rival Cornwall.

The Arena, Clinton, New York

The Hockey Mecca of Central New York

The original Clinton Arena on Kirkland Avenue was built in 1948 on the site of the present facility. It was destroyed by fire in September, 1953. A quonset-style wood frame building covered with aluminum sheeting, it was funded by a non-profit group who contributed $43,800 for its construction.

❦ The O'Brien family (Clinton, Franklin Springs) ❦

The cornerstone was laid for the present Clinton Arena on Kirkland Avenue in late 1953. Left to right on the platform: Ralph Allinger, WIBX sports announcer; Boyd Golder, Mayor of Utica; Edward Stanley, "Mr. Hockey"; Stanley Germond, local contractor; and Fred Goering, Mayor of Clinton.

This aerial view shows the present Clinton Arena in 1954. It remained the home of Clinton's professional ice hockey team, the Comets, until their demise in 1973. It is now called the Edward W. Stanley Recreation Center, honoring the man who spearheaded its rebuilding and who made Clinton "The Biggest Little Hockey Town in the U.S." (photo 1963)

❦ In memory of Edward W. Stanley — Melville & Evelyn Edwards & Fred Doyle ❦

62

Here's an aerial view of the Clinton Canning Company complex on McBride Avenue, with the New York Ontario & Western Railway tracks in the background. Built in 1892, the factory was in existence until 1937. The company canned produce grown by area farmers, primarily corn, peas, and green beans. During a peak harvest season, as many as 150 local people were employed in the production of thousands of cases of canned goods. "Clinton" in huge block letters was painted on the roof as a visual aid to early aircraft. Later, several of the buildings were used for the

manufacture of such varied products as plastics, hand tools, polishing compounds, and dog food. All the buildings have disappeared except for the elongated one near the right edge, which houses the Clinton bowling alleys. (photo 1939)

This winter view shows farmers leaving the William J. Cheney mill on Kirkland Avenue with loads of livestock feed. Purchased by Cheney in 1902, the mill was sold to W. H. Morse and his son Howard in 1927, and is now part of Agway. A section of the building was originally a Chenango Canal warehouse built in the 1840's and moved to this site in 1884 from a point close to the present-day Chenango and Kirkland Avenue intersection. (photo circa 1923)

❦ Chris & Barbara dedicate this page to Betty & Walter Blatz & Jeanne & John Doepp ❦

The Waterville-Clinton bus was in operation from 1912 to the middle 1920's. The company ran scheduled buses through Deansboro to Clinton, where they connected with Utica-Clinton streetcars at the South Park Row end of the village green. After discontinuance of the bus line, one of the buses was used to transport school students from Deansboro to the school on Marvin Street. (Before centralization, pupils from Deansboro attended high school in Clinton.) Incidentally, one of the students drove the bus. (photo circa 1920)

This photograph shows the Clinton Central School buses standing on the Kirkland Avenue lot, now the site of the Clinton Arena. Maintenance of school buses was then the responsibility of Gene M. Oliver, who operated a garage across the street in the building, now the headquarters of the Utica-Rome Bus Company. These school buses were painted with the school colors, maroon and white, a prevailing practice before New York State mandated all school buses be painted yellow. In the background is the Clinton Canning Company on McBride Avenue. (photo circa 1934)

❦ To Mary Lynn, Jean, and Kim Munson — Helen and Phil Munson ❦

In this scene looking south up Williams Street from the corner of College Street, you will note the boardwalk leading to White Seminary, the female department of the Clinton Liberal Institute. Both buildings shown in opposite corners of the photo were eventually destroyed by fire, the one on the left in 1876, the one on the right in 1879. (photo circa 1860)

This is a view of the Williams Street office of Dr. J. N. Garlinghouse, dentist. The building was built in 1876 by Dr. Garlinghouse's uncle, Dr. John A. Beardsley, whose office had been in the Mannering Block, which was destroyed by fire, along with the Presbyterian Church, that same year. Currently this building houses the dental practice of Dr. John F. Menard and Dr. James L. Francis, and thus has been a continuously-operating dental office for 117 years. (photo 1910)

❦ Compliments of James L. Francis, D.D.S. and John F. Menard, D.D.S. ❦

This is a view of tree-lined Williams Street looking toward Chestnut Street. The two houses visible in the right foreground were long known as the Hayes and Watrous homes. The first was built in the early 1850's by Ephroditus D. Thomas, a well-known boot and shoe manufacturer in early Clinton. He was a son-in-law of Erastus Barnes, Clinton's first potter. The home was purchased in 1888 by Cory D. Hayes, founder of the Hayes National Bank, and it was he who built the second of the two houses in 1905; this was long occupied by his daughter, Grace Hayes Watrous. (photo circa 1910)

This is the top of Williams Street looking toward the Chestnut Street corner and the imposing E. F. Torrey house. It's interesting to note that the site of this house was once briefly considered as a location for the public school erected on Marvin Street in 1893, and for the new St. Mary's Church erected 1910-13. (photo circa 1910)

❦ Compliments of Patsy and Dick Couper ❦

From the dip on Kellogg Street, looking west toward the Village Green, note West Park Row in the distance. (photo circa 1910)

New housing on Meadow Street (Route 12B) was built by local contractor John E. Pryor in 1925. (Today the Clinton Shopping Center stands across the road from these homes, to the left of the scene in the photo). It was John E. Pryor who, at this same time, developed streets off College Street, Sunset Drive, Berkley Drive, and Woodlawn Place. He also made the entry from College Street for Hamilton Place.

❦ Sponsored by the Beigel family ❦

The house in the right foreground, on the corner of Marvin and Chestnut Streets, was built in 1884 as a private school called Florence Seminary. From 1886 to 1889 it was another private school, Huntington Hall, and from 1891 was used as a public school until the Marvin Street Union School opened in 1893. From 1894 until about 1918 it was operated by Dr. George H. DeNike and his brother as a Gold Cure, an alcohol and drug abuse treatment center. In 1919, a large rear wing was removed and it became an apartment house. Today it's a private residence. (photo circa 1910)

Looking Down Marvin Street, Clinton, N. Y.

Dr. and Mrs. George R. Taylor, with son Bayard and daughter Bessie, are shown sitting in the driveway of their home at No. 2 Marvin Street in their new Paige automobile. The house, recently restored to the board and batten style from stucco, is today somewhat hidden by a business building at the corner of Marvin and College Streets. (photo 1906)

❦ Compliments of Charles and Cynthia Kershner ❦

The Brimfield Street mine was located a short distance above Dawes Avenue on the right side of Brimfield. The last active mine in the area, it closed in 1963. This mine, unlike the other local underground mines, had a vertical entrance where miners were lowered by an elevator of sorts to the mine shafts below. Ore from this mine was used exclusively by the Clinton Metallic Paint Co. for the manufacture of red paint pigments. (photo circa 1920)

This scene is at the Borst Mine, on Brimfield Street. Wagons of this sort with 4" wide treads were used to transport ore to the Franklin furnaces in Franklin Springs through Clinton village streets. Much to the concern of most residents, they not only dug up the roadway, but left a red residue that stained everything that came in contact with it. (photo circa 1890)

❦ Compliments of Pat and Doug Burrows, Jr. and family ❦

This is a view of workers surrounding the same Franklin Iron Works mine entrance shown in the photo below. During peak production, as many as two hundred men were employed. These mines closed for good in 1905.

The entrance to the Franklin Iron Works mine between New Street and Dawes Avenue is shown in this photo. The mine shafts that ran from this entrance honeycombed the area between Brimfield and Kellogg Streets, east of New Street. Ore was transported by mules hitched to small cars (like the one shown) to New York Ontario & Western Railway hopper cars on a railroad siding that ran from New Street across Utica Street to the main line tracks. There it was transported by trains to the Franklin blast furnaces and to others furnaces in New York State and Pennsylvania. (photo circa 1880)

❦ Compliments of Tom Bogan and Alice Root ❦

Opened about 1890 by Charles A. Borst, this iron ore mine was situated on Brimfield Street in the area behind and above the present-day Lutheran Home complex. Originally just a supplier of ore to the Clinton Metallic Paint Company, the operation was enlarged and modernized in 1903 to supply other users in New York and Pennsylvania. At this time, the New York Ontario & Western Railway constructed a rail siding from their main line which provided service to the mine. It was used

POWER PLANT, CLINTON HEMATITE IRON ORE MINES, CLINTON, N. Y.

to transport outgoing carloads of ore and incoming coal for the new power plant that not only furnished power for mining operations but electricity for the Village of Clinton. The entire operation closed soon after Mr. Borst's death in 1918.

It is believed that this view shows some of the clearing and leveling operation required at the original Borst mine prior to its upgrading in 1903. It's not ore being removed, but dirt to be used as fill elsewhere.

❦ Compliments of Don and Annette Foley ❦

This is a view of the Franklin Iron Works blast furnaces as they appeared in Franklin Springs around the turn of the last century. Located north of today's Route 12B between the Oriskany Creek and Furnace Street, they were demolished by the wrecker's ball in 1913. Constructed in 1850, they were enlarged in 1870 to produce 100 tons of pig iron per week, using about 350 tons of ore and 240 tons of coal. The ore was Clinton Hematite mined nearby. The blast furnaces operated sporadically until 1892. Note the springboard over the water in the furnace pond, (or dike, as it was called). At the time of the photo, it was being used as a swimming pool by area residents. (photo circa 1900)

After the closing of the furnaces, the dike was used for several years to harvest ice. Here, George Harrington, a local ice dealer, is cutting chunks to be stored for summertime use. (photo circa 1920)

❦ Compliments of Clayville Ice ❦

The Kirkland Blast Furnace was located on the westerly bank of the Oriskany Creek in Kirkland, near the present-day Route 5 bridge. It was opened in 1873 and operated sporadically until about 1890. It was demolished in 1913, the same year as the furnace company in Franklin Springs. Iron ore came from the Clinton mines as well as from strip mining operations in the Town of Westmoreland. (photo circa 1880)

Shown here is an interior view of the Franklin Iron Works, where workmen and visitors are about to witness the release of molten iron from the base of the furnace into sand molds in the foreground. (photo circa 1880)

❦ Compliments of Clinton Kiwanis Club ❦

The Red Mill Bridge, near Clinton, N. Y.

The so-called "First" Bridge spanned the Oriskany Creek on Dugway Road near present-day Sawyer Road. Just south of the bridge was a dam that from early days of settlement to the early part of this century furnished power at times to a nearby grist mill, as well as to other small enterprises: a chair factory, a triphammer shop, a saw mill, and a place that made cotton batting. The dam was destroyed by a spring freshet in 1902 and never rebuilt. The area around the bridge was variously known as Red Mill and Farmer's Mills. (photo circa 1912)

27—The Dugway, near Clinton, N. Y

This view of Dugway Road is not far from the "First" Bridge. The road probably got its name from that portion that hugs the shale cliff south of the bridge. One can surmise that early settlers to the south literally dug a path between the hill and the Oriskany Creek to reach the early mill near the bridge. Without such direct access, long detours would have been required to reach the spot. (photo circa 1908)

❧ Compliments of Helmuth-Ingalls American Legion Post 232 ❧

21—Street View at Franklin Springs, N. Y.

"Downtown" Franklin Springs about 1910 looked like this. Post Street bears to the left while present-day Route 12B bears to the right.

G. Wells Smith was an early owner of the Split Rock Mineral Springs on Dugway Road in Franklin Springs. Discovered in 1898, the spring was long a producer of mineral water, spring water, and soft drinks. It was the last of several in the area to close, shutting down in 1974.

❦ Compliments of Tim & Sue Suppe; Mary Rogers & Pat Donovan; Don & Julie Adams ❦

This gazebo on the farm of Frederick Suppe Sr., stands on the site of the first mineral spring discovered on Dugway Road in the summer of 1888. Given the trade name "Franklin," the spring was very successful for many years. One result of the mineral spring's development was the 1898 renaming of the post office, hamlet, and railroad station from Franklin Iron Works to Franklin Springs. The boy in the picture is Frederick Suppe, Jr., who later operated an automobile dealership on Utica Street, now the site of Nice N' Easy.

In this photo the spring house of Split Rock Mineral Springs on Dugway Road is shown with Mr. and Mrs. Arthur C. Suppe, then the proprietors, who operated it from 1912 to the 1950s. The well was discovered by Arthur Suppe's father, Charles F. Suppe, a brother of Frederick H. who opened the "Franklin" springs next door. It had several owners prior to Arthur Suppe. (photo circa 1921)

Clark Mills is "small town U.S.A.," the epitome of peace and tranquility. On the left, in the background, is Hooson's Service Station, first opened by Frank Hooson in 1928 and later run by sons Bill and Ken.
On the far right is Lynch's Store, operated for many years by Mary Lynch and her brother Tom. They sold the business on the eve of World War II and it became Acee's Market. Edward Meelan ran it from 1946 until 1985; it remains in business today,

BUSY CORNER, CLARK MILLS, N. Y.

operated by his son Bob. In the right foreground is James Nolan's Confectionery Store which opened in 1922. Prior to this, his father had operated the West Shore Hotel on the site. Nolan retired in December, 1976. Mr. Nolan once mailed one of these postcards to a Clark Mills resident serving with the US Navy aboard an aircraft carrier. When he showed the postcard to one of his shipmates, the other sailor exclaimed, "If that's busy, what's the rest of the town like?"

Clinton Street, showing Methodist Church, Clark Mills, N. Y.

The Methodist-Episcopal Church, located on then-unpaved Clinton Street, was the second church building erected in Clark Mills. The first pastor, the Rev. F. B. Stanford, circulated a subscription paper to institute a church building fund. A lot was purchased from J. W. French for $200 and construction began in 1895. Pastor Stanford drove his horse and wagon to nearby Oriskany Creek, and there, with his own hands, dug stones out of the creek bed and hauled them back for use in the foundation. The first actual church services took place in January, 1896.

In 1960 the edifice was beautifully modernized. The old bell was mounted on a masonry pedestal located on the front lawn. A large wooden cross, illuminated at night, was installed on the left front of the building. Now known as the United Methodist Church, it remains central to the community.

❦ Compliments of Tony and Tina Acee ❦

Church of The Annunciation, Clark Mills. N. Y.

The Church of the Annunciation is located on the south side of South Street. The third church in Clark Mills, it was constructed largely of materials from Clinton's White Seminary, which was dismantled, moved to Clark Mills, and essentially reconstructed. On Sunday May 8, 1910, the church was dedicated and celebrated its first mass. The Rev. James O'Reilly, the first pastor, was at the time also pastor of St. Mary's Church in Clinton and was instrumental in establishing the parish in Clark Mills.

A significant number of Clark Mills residents who were not Catholics assisted in bringing the project to a successful conclusion. The Church, with its parochial school to the rear on Clarey Avenue, remains very active to the present day.

EPISCOPAL CHURCH, Clark Mills, N. Y.

St. Mark's Church was the first to be erected in Clark Mills and remained the only one for more than thirty years. Prior to its construction, services had been held in the old schoolhouse on the east bank of the Oriskany Creek and the north side of what is now known as Main Street. The first service was held on Sunday, October 5, 1862, with the Rev. Russell Todd officiating.

The building was constructed by C. J. O. Kinney of Clark Mills on land donated by the A. B. Clark Company. The Right Reverend William H. Delancey, Bishop of the Episcopal Diocese of Western New York, laid the cornerstone on June 6, 1863, and later that year gave his consent to incorporate the parish. The parish was considered formally organized on November 17 and remains a vital institution to the present day.

78

This Clark Mills schoolhouse was on the north side of Main Street across from the Hind & Harrison Plush Company. It began around the turn of the century as a two-room school to which a third room was added around 1909. This room later housed the Clark Mills Branch of the Kirkland Town Library. The structure continued to expand, acquiring two more rooms in front and a small first-floor office. Miss Jackson taught 6th,7th and 8th grades and also served as principal. Several senior citizens who were her pupils fondly recall her today as "the best teacher" they ever had.

A second floor was added about the time of World War I. Comprised of one large room with a stage, it saw service as an auditorium and for a number of years housed the third and fourth grades, taught by the same teacher. The northeast room was the fifth grade, taught for many years by the late Agnes Fay. The northwest room was often used only for storage and activities, prior to centralization with Clinton in the early 1930's. The building was also the home of Clark Mills High School.

Graduating classes were extremely small, as many students had to leave before graduation to work in the mill and help support their families. The school, which then encompassed kindergarten through sixth grade, closed in 1957 when a new school opened on the "Old Cricket Field." The building was demolished in 1965, the land to become the site of the Firemen's Field Days.

On June 20, 1917 Clark Mills residents turned out for the dedication of the new flagpole with its distinctive eagle perched on top. Patriotic fervor ran high; a number of the area's young men had volunteered for military service in World War I, which the United States had entered two months earlier. But the pole proved to be too high! In a good wind it was observed to bend at the foundation and at the first joint. Concerned residents were forced to reduce the height by a full 25 feet.

In 1991 the eagle was beginning to show its age. A restoration committee crated the old bird and shipped it to San Diego, where metalsmith and former resident Jack Chidgey refinished the tarnished symbol free of charge. On Friday evening, June 21, 1991, the spruced-up eagle was rededicated, at which time the local women and men who served in Operation Desert Storm were welcomed home. Jack Chidgey was present and spoke briefly.

It is not recorded when the old bridge over the Oriskany Creek was built, or by whom. The year 1940 saw it replaced by a new steel one. The view on the postcard is looking north, with the home of Amos Hubbard partially visible on the left. The road to the right of the bridge is known as Main Street, whereas on the left or west bank, it is designated South Street.

BRIDGE ON ORISKNEY CREEK, Clark Mills, N. Y.

❧ Compliments of the Class of 1943 ❧

NEW BRIDGE, ARTHUR HIND CLUB AND POST OFFICE, CLARK MILLS, N. Y.

The "new" steel bridge enables Clark Mills residents and their visitors to cross the Oriskany Creek conveniently.

On the rear left we see the Arthur Hind Club. The second floor of this structure housed the Club Theater, which for many years showed first-run films, when flooding of the Oriskany Creek did not force its closing. American Legion Post #26 purchased the building in 1946. Memorial Day services are conducted every year on the lawn of this old landmark. The building immediately to the right of the bridge housed the Clark Mills Post Office and was also the location of Hoyland's Plumbing and later Barron's Plumbing. Freida's Restaurant also occupied part of the ground floor in the early 1950's. (photo circa 1913)

This is a view of Prospect Street, looking east, one of the last streets built by the Hind & Harrison Plush Company. Reportedly the workers who built these homes divided into two groups: one working from the intersection of Clinton Street; the other commencing from the other end. Old-timers claim that the houses in the middle were constructed with whatever materials were left over.

In the 1930's the plush company sold the houses on Prospect Street, along with many others in the community, to their occupants, many of whom were employees. Purchase prices were very modest, as the rents had been. The street has always been residential, save for Bramley's Kennels and, later, Fisher's Auto Glass Shop on the left corner. (photo circa 1920)

This, the Hind & Harrison Plush Company Main Building, was constructed in 1846 by the three sons of Noah Clark, textile brokers on the New York Stock Exchange. The structure boasted more than 110 looms by 1849. The number of looms grew and the output of cotton sheeting reached some two million yards by 1875. Childless, the Clarks left the factory to their cousins, Sweeney & Fitzsimmons. But the once-thriving business ground to a halt in 1890, leaving Clark Mills little more than a ghost town. At that time, Arthur Hind, an English industrialist, and his associate, a Mr. Harrison, purchased the facilities and began the manufacture of plush fabric calling the company the Hind & Harrison Plush Company. Hind & Harrison brought many of their employees from England with them, giving the community a distinctive English atmosphere which endured for many years.The venerable old factory still stands today, in active use as a warehouse, although the signs once atop the roof have long since been removed.

This photo shows a picturesque tower on the top center of the old Mill Building. Enchanting as the tower appears, it was probably added by an artist and never actually existed. (Not even the most senior Clark Mills residents can remember the tower ever being there.) Inside were located the company offices, including those of the "bosses" (they were not known as "managers" or "supervisors" in those days) and that of the owners, Arthur Hind, W. R. Kennish, and P.W. Copeland, during their respective times of company control.The plush company sold coal to village residents, and there was also an office where orders were taken, bills sent out, and payments received. By 1972, the long-closed building had deteriorated to the point that it was demolished.

82

View of Trolley Car at Clark Mills, N.Y.

The trolley shown in this postcard was more correctly known as an "interurban," since it was larger than a standard trolley car and operated between cities, rather than entirely within them. Interurbans were fast, frequent, safe, and economical and did not pollute the atmosphere. Service on the Oneida Railway, or Electrified West Shore, or Third Rail System (all three names were applicable) began on June 15, 1907 and continued until December 31, 1930, at which time the enterprise was abandoned. Clark Mills was an important stop and almost all eastbound cars (to Utica) and westbound cars (to Syracuse) stopped here.

Electric power was supplied to the cars through a shoe that came in contact with the third rail when operating on the main line. A pole on the roof came in contact with the overhead trolley wire, performing the same duty when the cars were within city limits.

WEST SHORE RR. DEPOT, CLARKS MILLS, N.Y.

For many people who immigrated from other countries and came to Clark Mills to work in the plush factory, their first glimpse of their new community was the West Shore Railroad Depot. Beginning in 1884 a number of steam trains of the New York, West Shore, and Buffalo Railroad (including the Albany Express, Buffalo Express and Canajoharie Local) stopped here. Later this line was purchased and operated by the New York Central Railroad. Between June, 1907, and December, 1930, the elegant Third Rail Trolleys (interurbans) stopped here, discharging and embarking travelers.

The West Shore station agent was also the Railway Express Agency agent and Western Union telegrapher. Local people could send and receive telegrams here. The station was closed about 1951 and torn down a few years later. The rails were taken up in 1965 and no railroad trains pass through Clark Mills today.

The New York, Ontario & Western Railway Station was located immediately to the east and slightly to the north of the Methodist Church. Clark Mills was a significant stop on the Rome and Clinton branch of the Ontario & Western Railway. Only 13 miles in length, the Rome & Clinton was built in the 1870's by a group of Clinton businessmen and operated until 1945 when it was sold. Passengers were not carried after 1931, although freight trains continued to rumble past until the demise of the Ontario & Western in 1957.

The station housed the Clark Mills Post Office for a number of years, until the post office relocated when the mail began to arrive by highway truck. The building was razed shortly after World War II.

Summer excursions by trolley car were frequently sponsored by the Hind & Harrison Plush Company for its employees. The destination was usually Sylvan Beach, which required those going on the "outing" to change to Ontario & Western steam trains at Oneida Castle. A charming, two-level station in that community accomodated both rail lines.

In those bygone days, innocent of air conditioning save the delightful breezes blowing through the windows when the cars

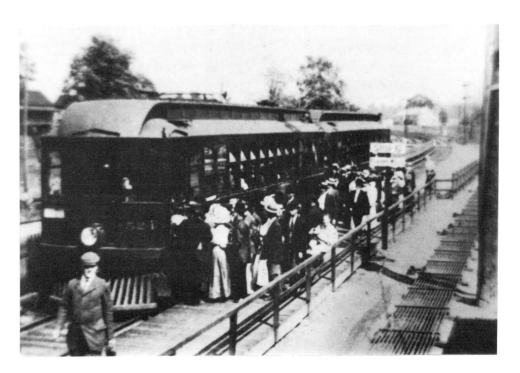

were in motion, the ladies wore long, heavy skirts and long-sleeved blouses, while the gentlemen attired themselves in suits and ties. Everyone wore a hat. While they must all have appeared well-dressed, they must have sweltered in the heat of a summer day. It was not uncommon for a person to faint. Discomfort notwithstanding, the excursions were usually well-attended.

❦ New Owls Inn -- Bernie & Jean Mahoney ❦

This postcard shows the hamlet of Kirkland as it appeared in the 1920's, looking east on Route 5. On the far left can be seen Grace Wood's store and the post office, followed by the Ed Lynch residence and then the Congregational church. This church was built in 1834. One of its longtime pastors, whom some may remember, was Clarence B. Post, who served from 1910-1934. Frequently, Hamilton College students assisted in the church services. The church was sold in 1966. (photo 1920)

The street we now call Old Bristol Road in Kirkland has had many names over the years, including Bristol Road, Lewis Street, Washington Road, and Maple Street, as shown above. In this shot we are facing Route 5. The first school in the District 2 area of Kirkland was built in 1834 near the corner on the left. This school was replaced by a new school built across the street, which still exists today as a residence.

❦ In Memory of William and Clara Fay ❦

This view of Route 5 in Kirkland, facing west, shows Glenn Dawes's hot dog stand next to the dance hall which was operated by his father Charles. Also in the picture is the Wheelock Tourist Home and lunch room. Across the street on the right is the Dawes residence, which was also a tourist home at that time.

The Dawes Place, Kirkland, N. Y.   8 Miles West of Utica on Utica-Syracuse Road

The residence of Mr. and Mrs. Charles Dawes on the corner of Route 5 and French Road was the former Pixley farm. When it was a tourist home in the 1920's, as many as thirty-two people could be accommodated overnight. The nine upstairs bedrooms still have the room numbers on them. In later years the Daweses became prominent area farmers.

The post office and feed and grocery store was operated by Gordon Grannis and his brother Floyd. Located on the corner of Route 5 and French Road, the building burned down in 1905. The fire, which started on a Sunday morning when many residents were attending the church nearby, scorched the adjacent Dawes home.

WILLOW REST, KIRKLAND, N.Y.   8 miles west of Utica

This view of the south side of Route 5 facing toward Utica shows the Willow Rest Tourist Home, which was owned and operated by Avery Wheelock. In the foreground is the lunch room with "pick-up" windows. Beyond is the Kirkland Dance Pavilion, built and managed by Charles Dawes. During the winter when basketball games were also held at the hall, visiting teams playing against Kirkland often came to Clark Mills by trolley and Mr. Dawes transported them with horses and bobsled.

❦ In Memoriam of the Grannis-Zumbrun families ❦

Along with the Kirkland Dance Hall, Danceland was one of two dance halls that flourished in Kirkland in the early 1920's. Live bands were featured and no alcoholic beverages were sold. Following a heavy snowstorm in 1925, the roof caved in, causing extensive damage. In later years the building became Harrison's Furniture Store and is now part of Serianni Antiques.

Ye-Ole Trolley Diner was a popular truck stop in the late 1920's and 1930's. Gas was sold and upstairs there were bunks open 24 hours a day for truck drivers. The diner was owned and operated by John and Pete DeCarlo. It later became Dowling's Tavern and is now unoccupied.

STITTVILLE CANNING CO., KIRKLAND, N.Y.

The Stittville Canning Company, located on Kirkland Avenue, later became the Haxton Company. This was one of several area factories that processed locally grown vegetables. The house on the left was the residence of the superintendent and his family, and the office on the right still stands on that spot. In the early 1920's, on the left of Kirkland Avenue near Route 5, Mr. and Mrs. William Kennett ran a large boarding house for factory workers.

" THE HOME OF FLOWERS " SENECA TURNPIKE, KIRKLAND, N.Y.

The Home of Flowers was the residence of Mr. and Mrs. S. Charles Grannis, who had a gardening business selling plants and cut flowers for over forty years at this location. A previous owner was L. D. Luke; after the death of his wife in 1883, he became a world traveler and wrote several books about his sojourns.

❦ Compliments "Birdies, Eagles & Ducks" — Mel and Sue Bonsel ❦

The office of the Stittville Canning Company was waterbound, as was Kirkland Avenue, during this spring flood. Part of this building still stands at George's Farm Produce. (photo circa 1920)

LIMBERLOST CABINS & MOTEL - Open Year Round - Kirkland, N.Y. - R. D. Clinton for Reservation

The Limberlost Cabins, built in the early 1920's, were typical of cabins of their era, forerunners of modern-day motels. Limberlost Road was originally part of the main highway from Syracuse to Utica. (photo circa 1955)

❦ Compliments of a friend ❦

HAMILTON COLLEGE

This drawing of Hamilton College gives a bird's eye view of the campus as it looked in the earliest years of the 20th century. Virtually all the buildings shown are still standing and in appropriate use.

This post-1940 aerial view of Hamilton's campus shows most of the same buildings, with the addition of the Alumni Gymnasium (1940) and the Sage Hockey Rink (1921) behind the pillared Root Hall to the left. The heart of the original campus, with its landmark Chapel, appears much the same today.

❦ Sponsored by Hamilton College ❦

Perry Hiram Smith Hall, now Minor Theater, opened its doors in 1872 as Hamilton's first library building. It was made of brick, in contrast to the college's earlier buildings of native stone construction, and named for an alumnus who had made his fortune in midwestern railroads and donated $13,000 toward the building's total cost of $25,000. It functioned as a library until superseded by the new James Library in 1914. Located on

50—Library, Hamilton College, Clinton, N. Y.

Campus Road, Smith Hall later served as the college infirmary, but was converted into a theater in 1962 through the generosity of Clark H. Minor, then chairman of Hamilton's Board of Trustees. The renovation project, which did not noticeably alter the exterior, was directed by well-known architect Edward Durell Stone. The college's theatrical productions continue to be staged in the building today.

This is an interior view of the original college library in Smith Hall, which had a capacity of 60,000 volumes but contained only 20,000, and had no catalogue and no scientific arrangement of books. Under the charge of a faculty member who served part-time as a librarian, it was for many years open to students for just eight hours a week.

❦ Sponsored by Hamilton College ❦

Looking down College Hill.

3746

College Hill and the steep, winding road that leads down to Clinton have long been part of Hamilton's folklore. Until the era of the automobile, the only alternative to struggling up by foot was a horse-drawn carriage or wagon, and it certainly helped students keep fit in the days before organized athletics or physical education programs. In contrast, going downhill was easy; the only thing needed was a sled. Students living in fraternities toward the bottom of the hill or in boarding houses in Clinton sledded down at meal times and at the end of the class day. It was a fast trip — from 40 to 50 miles an hour, depending on the size of the sled and number of occupants (from one to three). When most of the sleds had accumulated at the bottom of the hill, the freshmen, called "slimers," were expected to haul them back up for use once again by their "betters," the upperclassmen.

CLINTON HILL CLIMB - OCT. 14TH 1922.
OUT OF A POSSIBLE 4 FIRST PLACES IN STOCK CAR EVENTS, HUDSON AND ESSEX WON ALL
OUT OF A POSSIBLE 5 SECOND PLACES IN STOCK AND NON- STOCK EVENTS, HUDSON AND ESSEX —
— WON ALL.

In 1922 College Hill's dirt road was paved over with concrete, marking the triumph of the automobile. Even earlier, intrepid auto drivers had turned the road into something like a stock car racetrack. Commercial competition also entered into the races, as Hudsons and Essexes vied with other makes for victory in the uphill contests.

❦ In memory of Ted and Joan Gall — the Gall children❦

Freshman Hill, Hamilton College, Clinton, N.Y.

In the 19th century, Hamilton students, who boarded in the village of Clinton and walked up College Hill Road to the hilltop campus every day, identified sections of the road by classes in ascending order from Freshman to Senior Hill. Several of Hamilton's fraternities were located in frame structures along the road, and most of the buildings that still stand are now the property of the college. Remodeled into rented apartments, they now house faculty members and administrators.

Sophomore Hill, Hamilton College, Clinton, N.Y.

Handcolored.

❦ Compliments of the Smallen family: David, Ann, Steven, & Linda ❦

94

130—Res. Prof. F. M. Davenport, Clinton, N. Y.

The Davenport House, just above the first bend on the south side of College Hill Road, was built on orchard land in 1910 by Frederick Morgan Davenport, Maynard-Knox Professor of Law at Hamilton from 1904 to 1929. He pioneered in the teaching of the social sciences, especially political science, at the college. The onetime U.S. Congressman, long prominent in state and national politics, employed a New York architect, Arthur Jackson, to design the three-story wooden structure in the Queen Anne style and with projecting gables on each end. It was generously given to Hamilton by the Davenport family in 1955 to serve as the home of its presidents. The following year, President Robert W. McEwen moved in, and it has been the presidential residence ever since.

28—The Arbor, Clinton, N. Y.

The stone arbor, halfway up College Hill on the north side of the road, was erected on the site of an earlier wooden structure that had served as a resting place for generations of Hamilton students trudging up the steep hill from the village of Clinton. Built in 1894 as a memorial to John Newton Beach, Jr., a student who had died of a heart attack in the summer of his junior year, the stone arbor continues to provide a respite for the hearty traveler on foot in this age of the automobile. Ever since the arbor's construction, a college myth has persisted that the student it memorialized had lost his life in a sledding accident on the hill. That stubborn belief gains credence from the fact that students did indeed risk fatal injury by sledding down the Hill in the days before automobile traffic made such a venture impossible.

❦ Compliments of the Tobin Family ❦

Summer Residence of Hon. Elihu Root, Clinton, N. Y.

Elihu Root, distinguished statesman and Nobel laureate, was born on College Hill, and in 1893 he purchased this home, which had originally been built in 1817 for Theodore Strong, Hamilton's first professor of mathematics. Until his death at the age of 92 in 1937, Senator Root spent his summers here and took a great personal interest in its grounds and gardens. After his death, the gardens were lovingly maintained by his daughter Edith, who occupied the home with her husband, General Ulysses S. Grant III, grandson of the Civil War hero and U.S. President. Their daughters owned the property until 1979 when the college purchased it. Now on the National Register of Historic Places, the building is called the Elihu Root House and contains Hamilton's admission and financial aid offices.

"The Museum," now Buttrick Hall, was constructed in 1812, the year Hamilton was chartered. It was originally the college's Commons, or dining facility. In the years since, it has been variously used as a carpenter's shop, private home, science lecture hall and laboratory, geological museum ("The Cabinet"), and even as a firehouse. In 1845 it was the residence of Horatio Gates Buttrick, the college's superintendent of grounds and registrar.

13—The Museum, Hamilton College, Clinton, N. Y.

There, in a small second-floor bedroom, his daughter Nancy gave birth to her son, the future statesman Elihu Root. In 1874 the building was named Knox Hall of Natural History after James Knox, a Hamilton graduate and benefactor. In the 1880's it was "Victorianized," its simplicity of design giving way to "gingerbread" and ornate wooden gables, as seen in this photograph. In 1925 the Board of Trustees decided to restore the old building to its original lines. The wooden superstructure, including gables and dormer windows, were stripped from it, and in 1926 the restored building, renamed Buttrick Hall, became Hamilton's administrative center and meeting place for the trustees and faculty. Today it continues to house the office of Hamilton's president as well as the business operations of the college.

❦ Compliments of Douglas and Dare Thompson ❦

96

The main entrance to the Hamilton campus is between two stone gate posts on the north side of College Hill Road. On the other side are lands that once belonged to the Root family. In 1968, in a former apple orchard on part of those lands, a second campus was constructed for Kirkland College, Hamilton's newly created coordinate college for women. Ten years later, when Hamilton's trustees opted in favor of

Entrance to College Campus, Clinton, N. Y.

Handcolored.

coeducation, Kirkland was dissolved and its former campus became part of an enlarged Hamilton. In 1993 a new path between the two campuses was constructed and a student activities village built along it to link the campuses more closely together.

The Quadrangle, Hamilton College. Clinton, N. Y. 12-30-05

The original campus quadrangle is lined with the college's oldest buildings, including Buttrick Hall (1812, seen on the left) and the Chapel (1825-27, on the right). The major addition in this century has been the Burke Library (1972), constructed on the site of Truax Hall, glimpsed in the background of this scene.

❦ Mark Vacca, Hamilton College Class of 1992 ❦

In 1793 the missionary Samuel Kirkland presented his plan of education to President George Washington and Secretary of the Treasury Alexander Hamilton in Philadelphia, then the new nation's capital. The heart of the plan was a school for the children of the Oneida Indians as well as those of the white settlers who were then streaming into central New York from New England in search of new lands and opportunities in the wake of the American Revolution. Washington "expressed approbation," and Hamilton consented to be a trustee of the new school, to which he lent his name. The Hamilton-Oneida Academy was chartered soon thereafter and became Hamilton College in 1812. More than a century later, a statue of the college's namesake was dedicated. Commissioned as a gift to the college by Thomas R. Proctor, a Utica philanthropist, and sculpted by George T. Brewster, whose works include the Statue of Hope atop Rhode Island's capitol, it was erected in front of the College Chapel and unveiled in 1918. In bronze, the effigy of Hamilton stands perpetual guard over the campus and has become one of its notable landmarks.

South College (now South Residence Hall) was erected in 1907, on the site of "Old South," Hamilton's first dormitory building, which had been razed the year before. At the time,"New South" was described as having "unexcelled accommodations," including "bath-showers, fireplaces, electricity, . . . an ideal college hall. " Periodic modernizations, the latest in 1993, have kept it a popular residence for students lucky enough to draw a room in it as a result of the annual housing lottery.

New South College, Hamilton College, Clinton, N. Y.

Handcolored.

❦ *"Carissima" Mickey & Gil ('45) Adams* ❦

98

Silliman Hall, a brick and limestone fantasia with a copper roof on its tower, is Hamilton's most architecturally intriguing structure. It was said to have been designed by a man "who told everything he knew," and if it has a unifying style at all, it is Richardsonian Romanesque. Originally named for trustee and philanthropist Horace B. Silliman, who donated the funds for its construction in 1889, it flourished as the campus Y.M.C.A. building, a student religious social center, through World War I. In

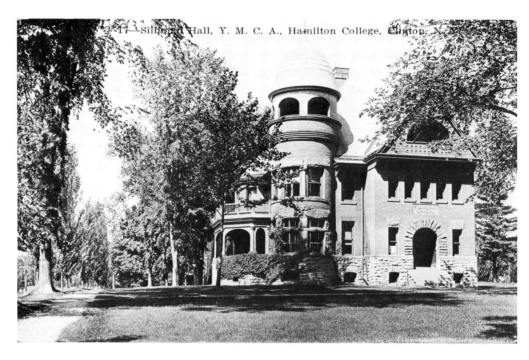

the 1920's Silliman Hall became the home of Hamilton's music department. It now contains offices and classrooms of the classics department and the women's studies and quantitative literacy programs. In 1992 it was rededicated as Couper Hall in memory of Edgar W. Couper, an alumnus and Binghamton businessman who became a leader in education as chancellor of the Board of Regents of the University of the State of New York.

From its early days, Hamilton has taken pride in its grounds. Rows of various trees such as elm, ash, maple, and poplar were planted to line its quadrangles and walks. In time they proliferated to the point that the once splendid view of the valley of the Oriskany was obscured. In the 1850's, influenced by Andrew Jackson Downing's *Treatise on the Theory and Practice of Landscape Gardening*, a committee set about

98—Campus Drive, Hamilton College, Clinton, N. Y.

systematically landscaping the campus with shrubs and trees, including oaks and evergreens, on the assumption that, in the words of the Rev. Amos D. Gridley, "It is no vain thing to suppose that the minds and hearts of students will be benefitted by daily walks through such grounds . . ."

133—The Chapel, Hamilton College, Clinton, N. Y.

Designed by the Albany architect Philip Hooker and completed in 1827, the College Chapel is among the most exquisite examples of a three-story, New England-style church still existing today. The college's preeminent landmark, it had long been the focus of religious life and student activities at the college. Until the 1960's, chapel attendance was mandatory and undergraduates were required to demonstrate their public speaking skills from the chapel's stage. In addition, the tolling of the chapel bell governed the college day, summoning students to and from classes. Until the triumph of electronics in the early 1950's, the bell was rung by relays of students, who slept nearby on the chapel's third floor. Today, the chapel remains a center not only for religious services but also for lectures, meetings, and special events such as reunions.

In the late 19th century the interior of Hamilton's chapel took on a heavy, gloomy, Victorian atmosphere when its original colonial simplicity was darkened by oak woodwork and stained glass windows (as seen here). After World War II, however, the building was restored to the spirit and style of the original chapel and dedicated to alumni who had died in the service of their country. Gleaming white became the primary interior color, and once again the grace of the exterior was matched by the austere inner beauty.

INTERIOR OF CHAPPEL, HAMILTON COLLEGE CLINTON N.Y.

❦ James Rishel, Hamilton College Class of 1974 ❦

The boundary line dividing the lands of the Six Nations of the Iroquois to the west and the colonists to the east was fixed before the American Revolution in the Treaty of Fort Stanwix (1768). During the war, the missionary Samuel Kirkland labored to keep the Iroquois from siding with the British and succeeded in persuading the Oneidas to maintain a friendly neutrality. In 1788, in recognition of his services on behalf of the revolutionary cause, he was jointly awarded a tract of land two miles square by the State of New York and the Oneida Indians. On what became College Hill just west of where the "property line" was located, he built his school, the Hamilton-Oneida Academy. The old boundary line, close to the bottom of the hill, was later marked by this granite shaft, erected by Hamilton's Class of 1887.

Stone marking the line of Property between the American Colonies and the Six Nations, fixed by treaty at Fort Stanwix, Nov. 5, 1768. Clinton, N. Y.

Chevaliers, J. C. White and Jay Keator at the Tomb of Chief Skenandoah of the Oneida Tribe, at Hamilton College, Clinton, N. Y.

The Oneida chieftain Skenandoah was a close friend and supporter of Samuel Kirkland in his missionary efforts, and led the delegation of Oneidas who were present at the laying of the cornerstone of the Hamilton-Oneida Academy by General von Steuben in 1794. Before his death in 1816, reputedly at the age of 110, Skenandoah requested that his grave be placed near Kirkland's, "so that I may cling to the skirts of his garments and go up with him at the great resurrection." They remained side by side in Kirkland's garden until 1856, when the remains of both were removed to the College Cemetery. Suitable monuments were erected to the two friends, now in their permanent resting place in adjacent plots.

❦ In Memoriam: Lillian Boyd Lewis by G. Harlan Lewis ❦

The Soper Hall of Commons, completed in 1903, was the gift of three brothers, chief of them an alumnus, Alexander Coburn Soper, who had prospered in the lumber business in Chicago after the Great Fire. The structure is in the Gothic style, with pointed windows and buttresses. So much does it resemble a church that students still circulate an old but baseless rumor that the donors originally intended it to be a house of worship but that the trustees had turned it into a dining hall instead. The rough exterior Gothic walls also pose an irresistible challenge to students with an urge to demonstrate their climbing prowess.

Hall of Commons, Hamilton College, Clinton, N. Y.

55—Interior Hall of Commons, Hamilton College, Clinton, N. Y.

The dining hall of Soper Commons measures 90 by 40 by 30 feet high. It continues to be one of Hamilton's three main dining halls, a place intimately familiar to virtually all living alumni. It has not changed drastically over the years, except that the paintings that once graced the walls have long since been taken down to prevent their being accidentally damaged by boisterous students.

❦ Compliments of Steve Sislo ❦

Hall of Languages, Hamilton College. Clinton, N. Y.

Benedict Hall, originally the Hall of Languages, was built in 1897 at a cost of some $25,000, thanks to the beneficence of alumnus Henry Harper Benedict. Along with partners, he purchased the Remington typewriter business from the arms manufacturing company and became the machine's chief salesman in Europe. Designed in the Romanesque style by Frederick H. Gouge, a Utica architect and also a Hamilton alumnus, Benedict Hall still serves its original function as a classroom building.

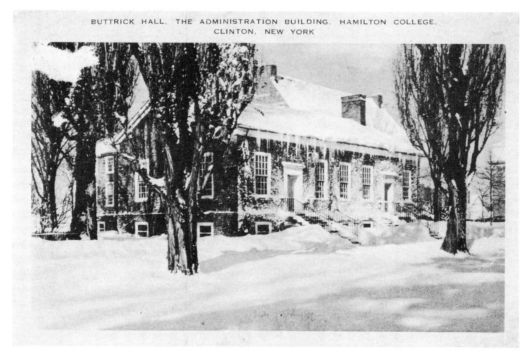

Buttrick Hall, the College's administration building, appears here much as it looks today, stripped of late 19th-century "Queen Anne" additions.

❦ Compliments of Tom and Jill Hebert ❦

The Well House, next to Buttrick Hall, was at first an open well used by students to draw water for the original Commons. Students continued to get drinking water from it (when they did not "lose" the bucket) into the present century. The "house" covering it was erected as a gift of the Class of 1897, and it remains in existence much as it appears here, although the well is no longer active.

2—The Well House, Hamilton College, Clinton, N. Y.

The college's second library was dedicated in 1914, the gift of an anonymous donor. At the ceremonies was Andrew Carnegie, on hand to receive an honorary degree. Many assumed that the Scottish-born millionaire, who lavishly dotted the land with libraries bearing his name, was the secret benefactor. Three years later it was revealed that Carnegie had not donated a dime, and that in fact the donor was Ellen Curtiss James, widow of copper king D. Willis James. The James

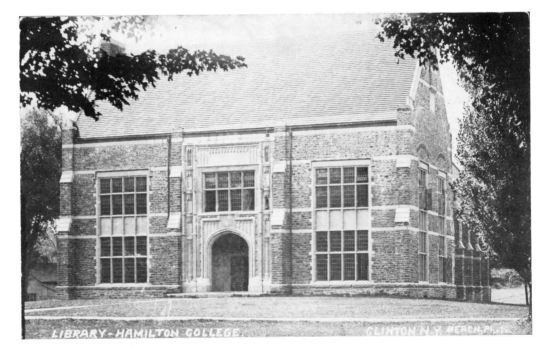

Library, designed by the Boston firm of Coolidge & Carlson and built in Tudor Gothic style at a cost of $123,000, had a vast main reading room resembling a medieval baronial hall with huge, ceiling-high windows to provide natural light. As the collection grew and the student population expanded, the building became inadequate and was abandoned for the new Burke Library in 1972. A decade later, the old James Library was drastically remodeled internally (necessitating sacrifice of the reading room), turned into classrooms, offices, and an art gallery, and rededicated as Christian A. Johnson Hall.

❦ Randy Whiting and Laurie Shaffer-Whiting, Hamilton Classes of 1982 & 1983 ❦

Truax Hall, called the Hall of Philosophy, was erected in 1900 at a cost of $27,000. The gift of alumnus Chauncey S. Truax, it was designed by Frederick H. Gouge of Utica, who had also done the somewhat similar Benedict Hall at the opposite end of Hamilton's main quadrangle. Truax Hall served as a classroom building and home of the History Department until 1971 when it was demolished to

Hall of Philosophy, Hamilton College. Clinton, N. Y.

provide the site for the new Burke Library. One of the few Hamilton buildings to be torn down in this century, its stately portico pillars now stand in the College Cemetery, where they add grace to the final resting place of generations of Hamilton presidents, faculty members, and alumni.

Hall of Science, Hamilton College, Clinton, N. Y.

Hamilton's main quadrangle formerly featured a campus fountain, the site of annual class tug-of-war contests and a dunking place for put-upon freshmen. When the noted theater critic, writer, and radio personality Alexander Woollcott was a student at the college, he was often thrown into the fountain. The story is told that once, when an elderly alumnus asked the water-soaked boy what Hamilton was preparing him to be in life, he replied, "a fish, you old fool, a fish."

❦ Sponsored by Cynthia and John Ellis ❦

8—Root Hall of Science, Hamilton College, Clinton, N. Y.

Root Hall, overlooking Hamilton's main quadrangle, was built in 1897 as the Hall of Science by Elihu Root in memory of his father Oren, professor of mathematics at the college. Costing $32,000 to construct and fronted by a porch with distinctive Ionic pillars, it was designed by the well-known New York architectural firm of Carrere & Hastings. Today it houses the offices and classrooms of the departments of English, comparative literature, and rhetoric and communication.

The north end of Hamilton's main quadrangle is still occupied by Sigma Phi Hall, home of the college's earliest fraternity, which was established in 1831. Destroyed by fire, the chapter house was rebuilt in 1917. Alongside it was the Litchfield Observatory, where the German-born Christian H. F. Peters, one of the most distinguished astronomers of the 19th century, discovered

Hamilton College. Clinton, N. Y.

numerous asteroids through his telescope in the days before photography was introduced as an aid to the naked eye. The observatory was torn down in 1918, but its outline impressed upon the ground is still visible from the top floor of the neighboring Burke Library during dry summer days. The central shaft of the old telescope now stands on the spot as a memorial to Peters.

❦ Compliments of Frank K. Lorenz ❦

The Chemistry Building was constructed in 1903 of local field stones and small boulders, and it is said that the true "architect" was the then-college-president, M. Woolsey Stryker. Although the "quaint and solid" structure was remodeled and enlarged in 1930, the original stones can still be seen under the newly added arches. It was again renovated in 1978 as the Saunders Hall of Chemistry. Named

Laboratory, Hamilton College. Clinton, N. Y.

for Professor Arthur Percy Saunders, a chemist but better known worldwide as a hybridizer of peonies, it continues to house Hamilton's chemistry classrooms and laboratories.

Hamilton's two oldest extant residence halls are North and Kirkland. Once called Middle College, Kirkland Hall (on the right) was originally built in 1821-25 and has undergone many renovations through the years. Transformed into a gymnasium in 1891, it reverted to a residence hall after 1940 when the new Alumni Gymnasium was constructed. Its last major renovation took place in 1962 when it was renamed in tribute to Samuel Kirkland.

❦ Professor & Mrs. Leland E. Cratty ❦

Russell Sage Bldg. "Hamilton College"

Hockey came to Hamilton in 1918 as a result of a coach's determination and a sense of national urgency. The coach was Albert I. Prettyman, the newly appointed athletic director, and the urgency was inspired by concern for the physical conditioning of men of military age after U.S. entry into the First World War. The first hockey games on College Hill were played on a slushy outdoor rink. Coach Prettyman began lobbying for an enclosed rink and succeeded in getting funds from a bequest of Mrs. Russell Sage, widow of a millionaire industrialist. Completed in 1921, Sage Rink, designed by the Utica architectural firm of Bagg & Newkirk, became the first and remains the oldest college indoor hockey facility in the country. The first game played in it, in January 1922, resulted in a 2-1 Hamilton victory over Amherst. The Hamilton Continentals have had their ups and downs over the years, but the Sage Rink, renovated in 1993, has never lost its icy charm for avid fans.

THE SCIENCE BUIDING BUILT IN 1925. HAMILTON COLLEGE. CLINTON. NEW YORK

Hamilton's Science Building, constructed in 1925 and expanded in 1965 with the addition of the Dana Wing, is the locale for student training in all the sciences except chemistry, which has its own building. Although it retains its original façade, the laboratory facilities and scientific equipment inside have been constantly upgraded. Through the years, many undergraduates who experimented as amateurs in its labs have gone on to distinguished careers. Pioneering sex therapist William H. Masters of the Masters and Johnson Institute is one such alumnus.

❧ In memory of Nicholas K. Burns, Sr. & Great friend Gregory Batt by Andrew C. Burns ❧

THE CLINTON CENTRAL SCHOOL DISTRICT FOUNDATION

"Quality" has always been the byword of the Clinton Central School District. That quality continues today with both the high school and the middle school having been recognized by the United States Department of Education as Schools of Excellence. Since it is becoming increasingly difficult to finance quality educational programs from traditional sources, the Board of Education created a Revenue Review Task Force to find supplemental funding sources for the Clinton Schools. The group concluded that forming a not-for-profit foundation would be one way to serve that purpose.

Based on that recommendation, the Clinton Central School District Foundation was established to ensure continuation of our tradition of excellence. The Board of Education chartered the Foundation in May of 1991 and appointed the four initial members of its Board of Directors. The stated purpose of the Foundation is to "supplement the funding of programs and projects which are already supported by public financing at a basic level, but which can be substantially improved and enhanced by additional private sector financing."

During its two-year history, the Foundation has sponsored several successful fund-raising activities: an annual antiques show, a Christmas wrapping paper sale, and a notepaper sale. Each of these projects was designed to draw from sources outside the local district and/or to provide something which would benefit district residents.

Working from this solid beginning, the Foundation expects that through continued efforts such as this pictorial history book, as well as an endowment trust, it will fulfill its mission and help Clinton Central School to continue providing an excellent education for our children.

James B. Torrance, Ph.D.
Superintendent of Schools

BOARD OF DIRECTORS

Douglas H. Burrows, Jr., President
Annette S. Foley, Vice President
Gwendolyn F. Foster, Secretary
Daniel Beigel, Treasurer

Margaret Adams   David Dupont
John B. Allen, Jr.   Christopher Fox
Roger Berkley   Dr. John F. Menard
Claire Burns   James Rishel
James Simpson

WITH SPECIAL THANKS TO OUR MAJOR SPONSORS

Savings Bank of Utica
Mr. and Mrs. Fred Alteri